ISBN 978-1-330-32880-4
PIBN 10029086

1 MONTH OF
FREE
READING

at
www.ForgottenBooks.com

By purchasing this book you are eligible for one month membership to ForgottenBooks.com, giving you unlimited access to our entire collection of over 1,000,000 titles via our web site and mobile apps.

To claim your free month visit:

www.forgottenbooks.com/free29086

English
Français
Deutsche
Italiano
Español
Português

www.forgottenbooks.com

Mythology Photography **Fiction**
Fishing Christianity **Art** Cooking
Essays Buddhism Freemasonry
Medicine **Biology** Music **Ancient**
Egypt Evolution Carpentry Physics
Dance Geology **Mathematics** Fitness
Shakespeare **Folklore** Yoga Marketing
Confidence Immortality Biographies
Poetry **Psychology** Witchcraft
Electronics Chemistry History **Law**
Accounting **Philosophy** Anthropology
Alchemy Drama Quantum Mechanics
Atheism Sexual Health **Ancient History**
Entrepreneurship Languages Sport
Paleontology Needlework Islam
Metaphysics Investment Archaeology
Parenting Statistics Criminology
Motivational

A GROUP OF FAMOUS WOMEN

STORIES OF THEIR LIVES

BY

EDITH HORTON

ILLUSTRATED

D. C. HEATH AND COMPANY, PUBLISHERS

BOSTON   NEW YORK   CHICAGO

TO THE
WOMEN TEACHERS OF AMERICA
WHOSE NOBLE LIVES HAVE EVER BEEN
AN INSPIRATION TO THE YOUTH
OF OUR LAND

FOREWORD

The best kind of American woman is proud. She has confidence in herself. She is not vain or conceited or self-assertive, but she has faith in her own powers. Even if she could, she would not spend her life in play or in idleness; she would choose to work. She believes that because she is doing her chosen work — whatever it may be — steadily, hour by hour, day by day, she is achieving. Because she has confidence in herself, she can live and labor serenely, proudly. No matter how obscure her lot, she feels herself to be in the same class as the most famous of her American sisters who have worked with steadiness and confidence at their task, and who have achieved greatness.

So difficult has it been for teachers to find brief, readable biographies of distinguished women to use in connection with their lessons in history and civics that they will welcome this interesting collection. It should help to make the girls in our American schools proud of their womanhood and it should give them a strong desire to be worthy of belonging to the same class as this group of noble workers.

EMMA L. JOHNSTON

Principal Brooklyn Training School for Teachers.

March 16, 1914.

"If women now sit on thrones, if the most beautiful painting in the world is of a mother and her child, if the image of a woman crowns the dome of the American Capitol, if in allegory and metaphor and painting and sculpture the highest ideals are women, it is because they have a right to be there. By all their drudgery and patience, by all their suffering and kindness, they have earned their right to be there."

— *O. T. Mason*

"The Egyptian people, wisest then of nations, gave to their Spirit of Wisdom the form of a woman; and into her hand, for a symbol, the weaver's shuttle."   — *John Ruskin*

INTRODUCTION

THE advantages of biography as a means of education are obvious. History and biography go hand in hand, the latter giving vitality and reality to the former.

Educators have for a long time appreciated this, and in many Courses of Study throughout our land provision has been made for the teaching of history through biography. In most cases, emphasis has been laid upon the notable careers of Washington, Franklin, Lincoln, and other illustrious men, with the purpose of interesting the young and inspiring in them the spirit of emulation.

It is a remarkable fact that little attention, if any, has been given to the study of the careers of distinguished women, and the question has often been asked why short biographies should not be prepared, in order that the pupils in our schools might become familiar with the noble and unselfish lives of the many remarkable women whose influence has been inspiring and uplifting. It is hoped that those who read the stories of the lives of the women whose names appear in this volume will find in them an incentive to guide their own lives into useful channels.

These types have been selected because of their direct influence upon events of world-wide significance. Only a limited number of types has been given because it would be impossible, within the compass of one volume or of many, to record the great and good deeds of women, past and present.

The compiler has no intention of expressing her personal opinions; the facts of these women's lives speak for themselves, and the stories, necessarily brief here, of their careers are so full of vital and human interest that it is hoped that the young reader may be led to the perusal of more complete biographies in later life.

INTRODUCTION

Many foreign born girls in our schools have practically no means of acquiring any adequate idea of the ideal standard of American womanhood — a standard radically different from that in their own native lands. The foreign born boys, however, invariably study the lives of great American men, and thus have no difficulty in familiarizing themselves with high ideals in ethics and statesmanship at precisely the time when the most enduring impressions are being made. As there is no reason whatever for this disparity of opportunity, it should cease, and by means of this little work and others of similar character, our school girls in general — and more especially those of foreign birth or parentage — should be made acquainted with the traditions and responsibilities of American women, and the unlimited opportunities for development and progress in this great Republic.

Women have been important factors in our national growth, and the value of their aid in carrying forward the progress of human improvement has never been properly estimated. The future of woman in America is undoubtedly to be of still greater significance to our country. Every art and profession is open to her, everything compatible with womanhood is within her reach, and she should be in readiness for the supreme civic privilege if such be granted her.

To-day, women are voting in ten states of the Union, a fact which calls attention to the necessity of educating girls for the duties of citizenship. The woman of the future will be better equipped to meet such duties by the study of the lives of certain representative women.

In the schools, side by side with boys, our girls study civics. Side by side with boys, they salute the Flag. Grown to womanhood, still side by side with men, they will help to uphold all the sacred traditions for which our Flag stands,— the true woman never forgetting that the home and the family are the bulwarks of the country.

E. H.

CONTENTS

LIST OF ILLUSTRATIONS

A GROUP OF FAMOUS WOMEN

"The woman's cause is man's; they rise or sink
Together, dwarf'd or godlike, bond or free."
— ALFRED TENNYSON

JOAN OF ARC: **THE PEASANT GIRL AT** DOMRÉMY

A GROUP OF FAMOUS WOMEN

JOAN OF ARC

(1410, 1412 – 1431)

"Oh child of France! Shepherdess, peasant girl! Trodden under foot by all around thèe, how I honor thy flashing intellect, quick as God's lightning, and true as God's lightning to its mark, that ran before France and laggard Europe by many a century, confounding the malice of the ensnarer, and making dumb the oracles of falsehood!"

— De Quincey

The story of the life of Joan of Arc is so unusual and so wonderful that it would be difficult to believe it to be true, if all that happened to her had not been told in a court of law and written down during her lifetime. Few facts in history come to us so directly, for these old records are still preserved in France, where they may be seen and read to-day.

Joan was born sometime between 1410 and 1412, in the little village of Domrémy, France, being the fifth child of Jacques and Isabelle d'Arc. Her parents were peasants in comfortable circumstances and Joan did not suffer through poverty.   She never learned to read or write — indeed, very few people at that time were able to do so — but she became skillful in the use of the needle and helped her mother in all the household tasks.   She was always good and obedient to her parents and kind to every one, especially the sick and the poor,

When work for the day was over, Joan ran about with her playmates, full of fun and frolic, dancing and singing for the pure joy of living.   Often the children would run to the beautiful forest near the village, where there was an oak which they called the fairy tree.   Here they would bring cakes for little feasts, at which they would dance, hanging garlands of flowers on the branches in honor of the good fairies.   This was a custom of peasant children of France in those days.

Joan would sometimes steal away from her companions and sit quietly and thoughtfully alone.   For she was living in a very unhappy time for France, and the misfortunes of her beloved country weighed upon her spirits.

Her father had told her of the sad condition of France, of how the kings of England had been for nearly a hundred years trying to make themselves kings of France, and how, little by little, they had taken possession of French lands until it was feared they would soon own the entire country and France would have an English king. Charles, called the Dauphin, son of the old French king, did not dare to be crowned, and no prince was thought to become really king of France until that ceremony had taken place. For centuries, the French kings had been crowned and anointed with sacred oil at the Cathedral of Rheims, but as the city of Rheims was far away and in the power of the English, Charles thought he could not safely go there.

As Joan grew older, she spent much of her time alone and in prayer, brooding over the wrongs of her country. She implored God to have pity on France. When about thirteen years of age, and while she was standing in her father's garden at noon one summer day, she suddenly saw a great light and heard voices telling her to be good, and telling her, also, that she must go to the rescue of her country. Joan said that she was only a young, ignorant peasant girl, who could neither ride a horse nor use a sword. But the voices kept on speaking to her for years, always telling her the same thing, to go to the relief of the Dauphin.

Joan at last came to believe that the visions and

the voices came from God, and she determined to obey them.   When she told her father and mother what she intended to do, they tried to dissuade her, telling her that the voices she heard were imaginary, and that it was impossible for a girl to do what trained military men and great generals had failed to accomplish.   Though it was very hard for her to act contrary to the wishes of her parents, Joan said she must do the work God had planned for her. Soon her gentle persistence had its effect, and people stopped laughing at her and ridiculing her, some even beginning to believe in her mission.

The voices bade Joan go to the Dauphin, who was then living at Chinon, a castle on the Loire, and tell him that she had come to lead his army to victory and that he would shortly go to Rheims to be crowned.

At first it seemed impossible for her to get to Chinon, but she went to Vaucouleurs, where her uncle lived, and with his help she succeeded in persuading Robert de Baudricourt, the commander there, to give her an escort of a few armed men for the journey. Someone gave her a beautiful war-horse, which, to the surprise of all, she rode well, though she had never ridden before in her life.   She cut her long, black hair short and dressed herself in doublet and hose like a boy, and this costume she wore during the remainder of her life.

On February 23, 1429, she rode out of Vaucouleurs through a gate which is standing to-day, and after several days journeying came to Chinon. Here there was some delay, for Charles was surrounded by people who advised him not to grant Joan an interview, but she was finally permitted to enter the great hall of the castle, where crowds of men, knights, and nobles in gorgeous attire, were assembled. But Joan was not dismayed. With confidence, but also with modesty, she walked up to one who was very plainly dressed, and fell on one knee before him saying, "God send you long life, gentle Dauphin." The man pointed to another, richly dressed in gold and silk embroidery, saying, "That is the King." But Joan said, "No, fair Sir!" She was not to be deceived, and her recognition of Charles, notwithstanding his disguise, caused all to wonder and many to believe in her.

The King asked her name and what she wanted.

"Fair Dauphin, my name is Jeanne the Maid; and the King of Heaven speaks unto you by me, saying that you shall be anointed and crowned at Rheims," Joan replied.

She then asked to be allowed to lead his army to the relief of Orleans, which city was under siege by the English at that time, telling him that under her guidance the victory would be theirs. Many of the nobles laughed at the idea of a girl leading an army, but after talking with her, Charles granted her request and sent her to Tours, where preparations were made for the journey to Orleans.

At length all was in readiness and the start was made. On a bright spring day, Joan rode away from Tours at the head of the King's army, wearing beautiful armor of white wrought iron. She carried an ancient sword, which she had divined was hidden behind the altar of St. Catherine in the chapel at Fierbois, and a banner embroidered with golden lilies. Such a sight was never seen before nor since.

It was night, April 29, when the French reached Orleans. They had safely passed an English fortress and entered the town without trouble. The people of Orleans, carrying torches, crowded around Joan, eager to see the brave girl who had come to their rescue. The women tried to kiss her hands and all the people shouted and cheered. The entire city rejoiced, for Joan's calm confidence, her bravery and decision, inspired the soldiers with belief in her and in the success of her undertaking.

Very soon Joan led her soldiers forth against the English and they were successful in taking several forts. She had prophesied long before this time that she would be wounded during the fighting, and one evening, shortly before the siege was raised, she said to Brother Pasquerel, the priest who was with her, "To-morrow rise even earlier than to-day. Stay always at my side, for to-morrow I shall have much ado — more than I have ever had, and to-morrow blood shall flow from my body."

The next day, while placing a ladder against a wall during the thick of the fight, a cross-bow entered her shoulder in spite of her armor and blood flowed. The arrow was drawn out and the wound was dressed, whereupon she insisted upon returning to the battle, though it is said she cried a little because of the pain.

At eight o'clock that night one of Joan's generals came to her for permission to stop the fighting until morning. But Joan asked him to wait a while. Then she rode into a vineyard and prayed. When she returned to the field, she found that a soldier had carried her banner into a ditch. She seized it, and waving it so that all the men saw it, cried, "When

my standard touches the wall, we shall take the fort!''
Soon the wind blew the fringe of the banner against
the wall and with a mad rush the French climbed into
the fort, while the English fled.

The next day, May 8, 1429, the siege was raised,
and ever since, the people of Orleans celebrate that
day and pay honor to Joan, called by them "The
Maid of Orleans."

Several other victories were won by the French
under Joan's leadership until the English were driven
far to the North.   Then Joan tried to induce Charles
to go to Rheims to be crowned, so that the French
people would feel that he was really their King.
But the distance was great and the roads passed
through towns which were occupied by friends of
the English, and Charles, who loved his ease, was
hard to move.   At length, however, he was persuaded, and with an army of twelve thousand men
Charles started on his journey to Rheims, which
city he entered on July 16, being crowned the next
day with imposing ceremonies.

This was perhaps the happiest day of Joan's life.
The great Cathedral was crowded with people, only
the center aisle being kept free for the procession.
First came the Archbishop, accompanied by his

canons in their robes of state. Then came men of high rank, magnificently dressed. From the west door Joan and the King appeared side by side, and cheers and cries of welcome greeted them, followed by a deep silence preceding the solemnity of the coronation. The Archbishop of Rheims administered the coronation oath; then the Dauphin was anointed with the sacred oil, and crowned, while the trumpeters played and the people shouted. The Maid knelt at the King's feet and wept for joy.

When asked by Charles to choose a gift as a reward for her work for her country, she begged that the people of her native town Domrémy might be free from paying taxes. This was granted, and for three hundred years the taxes were remitted. On the books is written against the town of Domrémy: "Nothing. For the sake of the Maid."

This was all Joan would accept. For herself she desired nothing except to be allowed to go back to her village home to tend her sheep and be again with her mother. But Charles VII would not consent to that, for France was not yet free from the English.

So it was decided to try to recapture Paris. Shameful to say, however, the King did not give Joan the assistance he should, withdrawing instead from the city. Soon afterwards, while leading an attack against the Duke of Burgundy, Joan was taken prisoner and sold to the English. King Charles made no effort to effect a ransom for her, nor did any-one else in France attempt to raise money to save her from her unhappy fate. She was charged with sorcery, put into prison in Rouen, and after a year was brought to trial. At the trial she was found guilty, was sentenced to death, and burned at the stake in the market place of Rouen, May 30, 1431.

Joan of Arc had no grave; her ashes were thrown into the Seine. There remains no relic of her, no portrait, or any article she ever touched. Still she will never be forgotten. It is now nearly five hun-dred years since her death, yet to-day she is honored and reverenced, and many statues have been erected to her memory.

A mere child in years, she rescued her country from the English by a series of brilliant victories, crowned the French king, and in return for this was burned alive at the stake, while those for whom she had fought looked on, making no effort to save her. She was seventeen years of age when she led the armies of France to victory, and but nineteen when she met her cruel death.

Her pure, steadfast, simple faith, together with her devotion to God and her patriotism, constitute her greatness. During her life in camp, in Court, in

her home, and in prison, she never forgot her womanly ideals, though she was called upon to do a man's work; and she stands to-day to all nations a shining example of pure and noble womanhood.

DOROTHY PAYNE MADISON

DOROTHY PAYNE MADISON

(1772–1849)

"It is by woman that Nature writes on the hearts of men."
— *Richard Brinsley* Sheridan

Dollie Madison was born May 27, 1772, in North Carolina. Her father, John Payne, was a native of Virginia, but he lived on a large plantation in North Carolina which had been given him by his father. He married Mary Coles, a noted belle and beauty, and their daughter Dorothy inherited her mother's good looks.

In their home on the Southern plantation, the Paynes avoided all display, although they enjoyed every comfort and were generous in hospitality. The little Dorothy was brought up to dress quietly and wear no finery. After their removal to Philadelphia, which occurred when Dorothy was fourteen years of age, both John Payne and his wife, already Quakers, became more strict in that creed than they had been before. It was Mr. Payne's conviction — as it was of all Quakers in good and regular standing

13

— that slavery was sinful, and this belief led him to free his slaves, sell his plantation and come North.

In their Northern home, the Quaker rules were rigidly carried out. Though young and of a particularly gay and joyous disposition, Dorothy — or "Dollie" as her friends called her — was forbidden such pleasures as dancing, music, and many other amusements. All this discipline, which we should call unnatural, Dollie received with sweetness and cheerfulness. Her beautiful face reflected a beautiful character.

Mr. Payne, who was untrained in business ways, met with financial reverses, and in his troubles was aided by a young lawyer of wealth named John Tod, also a member of the Society of Friends. This young man, who had fallen in love with Dollie, showed Mr. Payne much kindness, finally obtaining his consent to ask his daughter's hand in marriage. When he proposed to Dorothy, however, she replied that she "never meant to marry." But her father was ill at the time, and to please him, Dorothy, like the dutiful daughter she had always been, consented, and so had the satisfaction of making her father happy for the remaining few months of his life.

After her marriage, Dollie lived for three years

the life of a Quaker matron, devoting herself to her husband, her home, and her two babies. Then an epidemic of yellow fever broke out, and John Tod sent Dollie and the babies away from the city while he remained to look after his parents, who were both dying of the fever.

As soon as he could leave, and already ill, he hastened to his wife and children. Mrs. Payne, Dollie's mother, opened the door for him. "I feel the fever in my veins," he gasped, "but I must see her once more!" In a few hours, he and one of the babies were dead. Dollie herself was then stricken, and fatally, it was believed. She recovered, however, and taking with her the remaining child, a boy whom she had named John Payne after her father, Dollie went to her mother in Philadelphia.

These sad experiences broadened and deepened her lovely nature so that she developed from a shy girl into an attractive woman. Her troubles seemed only to increase the natural sweetness of her disposition and enhance her beauty. These gifts, together with her youth and riches, caused her to become the object of much curiosity and attention.

On a certain morning during her walk, she was seen by James Madison, who immediately sought for an introduction. This undoubtedly flattered Dollie, for Mr. Madison was a very prominent and important figure in Congress, with a name celebrated throughout Europe and America. He had worked with Washington, Franklin, and Hamilton to establish the United States government on a firm basis, so that he has since been called the Father of the Constitution.

In a letter to her friend Mrs. Lee, Dollie wrote:

DEAR FRIEND:

Thou must come to me. Aaron Burr says that the "great-little Madison" has asked to be brought to see me this evening. . . .   .

When he came, Mrs. Tod received him in a fine mulberry satin gown, with silk tulle about her neck and a dainty lace cap on her head, a curl of her pretty black hair showing from underneath. She so sparkled with fun and wit that the scholarly Mr. Madison concluded that there was nothing to do but to offer himself as a husband, and before long they became engaged.

President and Mrs. Washington were much pleased when they heard of this and sent for Dollie to come to them. Mrs. Washington said, "Be not ashamed to confess it, if it is so," for Dollie was shy and confused. ` Then she added,

"He will make thee a good husband and all the better for being so much older. We both approve of it. The esteem and friendship existing between Mr. Madison and my husband is very great and we would wish thee to be happy."

Dollie was just twenty-two years of age and Mr. Madison forty-four. In September, 1794, at Harewood, Virginia, the home of Dollie's sister who had become the wife of a nephew of Washington, Mrs. Tod and James Madison were married. The guests came from far and near, and there was much merrymaking and gaiety at the wedding; even the quiet, reserved bridegroom became transformed and permitted the girls to cut off bits of Mechlin lace from his ruffled shirt as mementoes.

The bride and groom went first to Montpelier, Virginia, Mr. Madison's home, but soon returned to Philadelphia, where, at the request of her husband, Dollie, laying aside her Quaker dress, entered society and began to entertain largely. Her tact and kindness of heart won every one, and at a time when party spirit ran high and political differences caused bitter feeling, Mrs. Madison entertained with dignity and elegance, slighting no one, hurting the feelings of none, and sometimes making friends out of foes.

When Washington died, Mr. and Mrs. Madison were among his sincere mourners, and helped to comfort the lonely widow for the loss of her great-hearted husband. When Thomas Jefferson became President of the United States, James Madison was made Secretary of State. Mr. Jefferson, being a widower, and requiring a lady to assist at his state banquets, often called upon Mrs. Madison to sit at the head of his table in the White House. Her charms especially fitted her for such a position.

After Jefferson had served two terms as President, James Madison was elected to fill his place. At the inauguration ball Mrs. Madison wore a gown of buff-colored velvet, a turban with a bird of paradise plume on her head, and pearls on her beautiful neck and arms.

During the first years of Madison's administration, while national affairs were going on smoothly, Mrs. Madison's entertainments at the White House were many and popular. She had the rare gift never to forget a name and the faculty of putting people at their ease, and thus banishing shyness and stiffness. Her receptions were never dull. Her sparkling conversation drew the best minds to her, and the ease with which she met strangers was remarkable.

She was kind alike to rich and poor, and gave generously of her wealth to the deserving.   To her husband she was an able adviser, her sound common sense and good judgment often helping him in his decisions of public matters.   President Madison said that, when he was tired and worn out from matters of state, a visit to his wife's sitting-room never failed to rest him.

But national affairs were not to remain quiet. Trouble had long been brewing with England.   The commerce of the United States had been almost entirely destroyed by acts of the British.   The Atlantic coast from north to south was blockaded by them and many American seamen were impressed.   Washington and Adams had managed to avert this war, but now matters were come to a crisis: the whole nation was inflamed, and on June 18, 1812, Congress formally declared war.

As most of the fighting was done at sea, life at the capital went on undisturbed until August 19th, when it began to be rumored that the British were coming to attack Washington. The rumor became a certainty when a horseman dashed through the villages forty miles below Washington, shouting:

"To arms!   Cockburn is coming!"

The English had landed five thousand men and were marching toward the capital. Washington was in a state of panic. Citizens banded together for defence and marched to meet the enemy. On August 22, President Madison bade farewell to his wife and left for the front. Up to this time Mrs. Madison had been without fear, but now, learning that the American ships had been destroyed and knowing that her husband was in danger, she became very uneasy.

The work of saving records was at once begun. Important papers were piled into wheelbarrows and carts and carried away. At three o'clock, August 24, Mrs. Madison sat anxiously waiting for some word from her husband. She refused to leave the White House until a large portrait of General Washington was saved, and time being too short to admit of its being unscrewed from the wall, she gave the order to have the frame broken with an axe and the canvas taken out. It was sent in a carriage to a woman living beyond Georgetown, who afterward returned it to Mrs. Madison. It now hangs in the White House again.

A hurried note from the President bade her be in

readiness to leave in a carriage at a moment's notice, for it was feared the British would destroy the city. Soon her worst fears were realized, for sounds of approaching troops were heard. Two gentlemen rushed into the room, exclaiming:

"Fly, madam! At once! The British are upon us!"

Mrs. Madison suddenly remembered that the Declaration of Independence, which was kept in a case separate from other documents, had been overlooked when the other papers were sent away. She turned, and notwithstanding the protests of her friends, ran into the house, broke the glass in the case, secured the Declaration, and then jumped into the carriage, which took her to the home of a friend in Georgetown.

Washington could be rebuilt and many valuable articles which were destroyed could be replaced, but the Declaration of Independence once gone would have been lost forever.

That night, few people in or near the city of Washington slept. Instead, they watched the flames destroying the beautiful city, for the British had set fire to the public buildings, the President's house, the new Capitol, the Library of Congress, the Treasury

Buildings, the Arsenal and Barracks, besides many private buildings, and the wind from an approaching storm fanned the flames, thus completing the fearful destruction.

Before daybreak, Mrs. Madison left her retreat and traveled to a small tavern, sixteen miles from Washington, where her husband met her. Shortly, word was brought to them that the hiding place of the President had been discovered, and that the British were even then in pursuit of him. Mrs. Madison induced him to retreat at once to a small house in the woods, while she started for Washington, first disguising herself, for the English had said that they were going to capture the beautiful woman and take her to England.

President Madison, however, learning that the British had evacuated Washington, returned to the city that night. His wife had also reached there in safety. The burning of Washington filled the hearts of Americans with indignation, and even in England many condemned the act of Admiral Cockburn, saying that it was "a return to barbaric times."

After three years of fierce conflict, the peace treaty between England and the United States was signed at Ghent, on December 24, 1814. Every one was glad, but no one more so than President Madison, who had been drawn by his party into the war and who was greatly criticized and blamed for it. The President and his wife now took a large house on Pennsylvania Avenue. The brilliancy of social life at the White House had never been equaled before Dollie Madison's time, and it is doubtful if it has been since.

In 1817, James Monroe became President and Mr. Madison retired to Montpelier, Virginia, where he and his wife entertained with true Virginian hospitality the many friends and tourists who came to visit them. Their home was a beautiful one, containing many artistic treasures. Here they lived happily until Mr. Madison's death in 1836.

Soon after her husband's death, Mrs. Madison returned to Washington to live among her old friends, and after a time her home again became a social center. Much consideration was shown her by Congress and by high officials, who respected her for her worthy and honorable life, and for her heroism during the burning of Washington.

During her latter years she was saddened by the dissolute habits of her only son, Payne Tod, whose debts had been frequently paid by President Madison and who now appealed to his mother for money. To save him from disgrace she even sold her beloved Montpelier.

Dollie Madison died in Washington, July 12, 1849, at the age of eighty-two, and was buried in the cemetery at Montpelier beside her husband.

Lossing says: "Mrs. Madison adorned every station in life in which she was placed."

MRS. FRY READING TO THE PRISONERS IN NEWGATE PRISON

From an old engraving

ELIZABETH FRY

(1780 – 1845)

"A lamp is lit in woman's eyes
That souls, else lost on earth,
Remember angels by."

— *N. P. Willis.*

In Warwick, England, lived a family of Quakers named Gurney. They were not "plain Quakers" at that time, which means that they did not wear plain clothes and refrain from the use of ornaments, nor did they refuse to take part in the pleasures of the world, as strict Quakers are supposed to do. The children, nevertheless, were brought up in accordance with the doctrines of the Bible, very rigidly inter-preted.

Mrs. Gurney, a woman of fine education and sound judgment, instructed her little daughters in English, mathematics, literature, Latin and French, and in do-mestic duties. They were taught to sew and to make plain garments, to oversee the preparation of the meals, and if necessary, to do the cooking. Very

27

great care was taken with their manners, for Mrs. Gurney believed that gentleness and polite behavior were necessary in women.

Elizabeth, the third child, born May 21, 1780, who became the famous Elizabeth Fry, was frail in health, and so nervous that she was afraid of the dark. To cure her of this, her father compelled her to go to bed without a light — a treatment that only increased her nervousness and fear. So firmly was the memory of this severe punishment fixed in the child's mind that, when she married and had children of her own, she never permitted any method of discipline that tended to cause fear.

Elizabeth had not a tractable disposition, but was inclined to be wilful, obstinate, and opinionated. Even as a child, she would act independently. This pronounced trait in her character, so objectionable in youth, enabled her in later years to do many things worth while, in the face of unreasonable opposition.

Her mother died when Elizabeth was twelve years old. As she grew older, she gradually broke loose from her Quaker training and began to think more about dress and adornments; she even learned to dance, and enjoyed going into society. But, while enjoying these pleasures, she all the while realized that she was not really happy. Then she tried to find out the reason. She went among the poor and helped them, but this was no more than all Quakers did. She feared that she was becoming more and more satisfied with the light, pleasant, easy things of life, while the great and good things that might be done ever haunted her, and called to her to regard them.

At this time a traveling Quaker preacher named William Savery, a man of great force and a powerful and compelling speaker, came over from America. He addressed a meeting of Friends which the Gurney sisters attended, including Elizabeth, all sitting in a row on the women's side in the Meeting-House. These young girls wore some ornaments and were more elaborately dressed than the other Quaker girls. When the speaker touched on this matter of adornment and in a gentle, tender voice pleaded for the customs of the plain Quakers, Elizabeth was much affected; all her pleasures seemed to her sinful, and she wept bitterly.

Afterward she had long talks with William Savery, in the course of which, it is said, he prophesied her future. His words changed Elizabeth utterly; she cared no more for the world and its pleasures.

Her father, to test the genuineness of her conversion, induced her to visit friends in London who lived in the midst of gaiety. There, she attended the theater, but was not interested; she danced, but found it dreary; she played cards, but was wearied. All the enjoyments of former times failed to satisfy her. She returned home, and after several months spent in meditation, finally came to the conclusion that, for her at least, those things were wrong; that, for her, life held more important duties. She then gave up all amusements, began to use the "thee" and "thou" of the strict sect, adopted the close cap and plain kerchief of the Quakeress, and preached at meetings.

Once her mind had cleared, she never wavered in the belief that her life must be devoted to works of charity. She began by opening a school for poor children. She was only nineteen, very youthful-looking and very pretty. Everybody wondered how she could govern this school of seventy wild street-children, who had never before known restraint.

While she was occupied with this school, a young Quaker from London, named Joseph Fry, fell in love with her and proposed marriage. At first Elizabeth thought she could not accept Joseph's offer; that to marry would interfere with her plans. But the young man was deeply interested in benevolent work, himself, and had sufficient means to assist her in her projects.

So they were married at Norwich, and later their home at St. Mildred's Court, London, became a meeting place for Quakers from all parts of the world. Instead of card-games and dancing for their entertainment, the visitors in this house heard discussions of plans for the formation of poorhouses, schools, and hospitals for the poor.

In 1809, Elizabeth's father died; and on her knees by his bedside, Elizabeth again vowed to devote her life to the service of God. She now lived in Plashet, Essex, the country seat of her husband's family. With growing children of her own about her and great numbers of guests, one might suppose that she had all she could possibly do. Nevertheless, she found time to open a girls' school for street-children, to organize a soup kitchen, a drug-store, and a library for them, while in her own home she kept a collection of clothes of all sorts with which to clothe them.

When this enterprise was well established and the poor people about her made comfortable, Mrs. Fry turned her attention to the great prison at Newgate, London, where conditions were reported to be shocking. In company with officials and a party of friends, she made her first visit, in 1813. They found things much worse than they had been led to believe.

Mrs. Fry at once determined to reform prison life. Illness in the family delayed this project for nearly three years; but the idea never left her until at last the work was begun. The life of the prisoners in Newgate, and in all prisons at that time, was too harrowing to be here described.

The public listened to her reports, were properly shocked, but scoffed at the bare idea of Elizabeth Fry as a reformer. For a *woman* to attempt such a work was absurd! Mrs. Fry paid no attention to what was said, but went straight ahead. She began by establishing a school for the prisoners' children, and gave the wretched women prisoners work for which they were paid. Before this, being idle, they had spent their time quarreling, fighting and gambling; now, when they could earn a little money, their behavior began to improve.

Soon Parliament took an interest in this work, ordering an investigation. When the wonderful reforms she had accomplished became known, Mrs.

Fry was the most famous woman in England. Queen Victoria expressed a desire to become acquainted with her, and a meeting was arranged which has been described as follows:

> Her Majesty's small figure, her dress ablaze with diamonds, her courtesy and kindness as she spoke to the now celebrated Quakeress, who stood outwardly calm in the costume of her creed and just a little flushed with the unwonted excitement, attracted universal homage. The two women spoke, and cheer after cheer went up from the crowd gathered about.

The Court learned that day that there was in goodness and benevolence something better than fashion and nobler than rank.

Mrs. Fry's work for the poor and unfortunate took her to the prisons of many lands, and everywhere honors were bestowed upon her. She died at the age of sixty, October 13, 1845.

LUCRETIA MOTT

LUCRETIA MOTT

(1793 – 1880)

"There is in every true woman's heart a spark of heavenly fire which beams and blazes in the dark hours of adversity."
— *Washington Irving*

Born on the quaint little island of Nantucket, January 3, 1793, Lucretia Coffin grew to girlhood among peaceful and beautiful surroundings. Her father was Captain of a whaler and was, consequently, often away from home for long periods of time, so that the mother was responsible for the early training of the children.

Lucretia and her sisters were taught to be thrifty in household matters, and trustworthy in all the relations of life. Industry, too, was greatly encouraged in the Coffin family. When the mother had to go out, she would set her daughters at their knitting, telling them that when they had accomplished a certain amount of work, they might go down into the cellar and pick out as many of the small potatoes as they wanted, and roast them. This was

considered a great treat, and we can picture the six
little children gathered about the big fireplace watching the potatoes in the ashes.

Captain Coffin gave up the sea at last and moved
his family to Boston, where he entered into business.
The children at first attended a private school, but
Captain Coffin, who was nothing if not democratic,
decided afterward that they should go to the public
school, where they might "mingle with all classes
without distinction." Lucretia said in after life
that she was glad of this action of her father. "It
gave me a feeling of sympathy for the patient and
struggling poor, whom but for this experience, I
might never have known."

At thirteen years of age, Lucretia was sent to a
Friends' boarding school at Nine Partners, New York.
Both boys and girls attended this school, but were
not permitted to speak to each other unless they
were near relatives. In that case they might talk
together a little while, on certain days, over a corner
of the fence that divided the playgrounds.

One of Lucretia's sisters — "the desirable little
Elizabeth," as her father called her — accompanied
her to this school. These sisters, although very
different in character, loved each other with a pecul-

iarly deep affection. Elizabeth, though clever, was retiring in disposition and always kept in the background, while Lucretia, who was high-spirited and wide awake, was inclined to take the lead among her companions. Throughout their lives they remained devoted friends, and although Elizabeth could never be persuaded to take any part in public life, she counseled and advised her distinguished sister, who seldom took any important action without consulting her.

At this school, on the boys' side of the house, was an able young teacher named James Mott. It happened one day that a little boy, a cousin of James Mott, was punished by being confined in a dark closet, being allowed only bread and water for his supper. Lucretia, who thought the boy had not been at fault, managed to get some bread and butter to him. This act attracted the attention of James Mott to the girl, and afterward his sister Sarah, who also attended the school, became Lucretia's most intimate friend. During one of the vacations, Lucretia visited Sarah Mott and thus met the family into which she afterward married.

When fifteen years old, Lucretia became assistant teacher in this school, at a salary of one hundred dollars a year. Her father, who thought women should be trained to usefulness, gave his consent to have Lucretia remain away from home for this extra year, which proved to be an eventful one for her. The two young teachers, James Mott and Lucretia Coffin, found that they had many ideas in common. Both had ability and both were desirous of gaining knowledge. They formed a French class and it was while studying together that their attachment began.

It was at this time, also, that Lucretia became impressed with the unequal condition of women as compared with that of men. She said:

"Learning that the charge for the tuition of girls was the same as that for boys, and that when they became teachers, women received only half as much as men for their services, the injustice of this distinction was so apparent that I early resolved to claim for myself all that an impartial Creator had bestowed." She little thought at the time what an important part she would play in supporting that claim.

While the two sisters were at school, their father gave up his business in Boston and took charge of a factory in Philadelphia, where Lucretia and Elizabeth joined him in 1810. Soon after, James Mott

resigned his position as teacher and followed them to
Philadelphia, entering business life.   In a short time,
he and Lucretia became engaged.   These two young
people were just different enough to live in harmony
together.

Lucretia was a bright, active and very pretty girl,
quick to understand and quick to execute, — qualities that often made her impatient with the slowness
or stupidity of others.   She was fond of a joke, too.

James, on the other hand, was quiet, reserved and
shy, taking serious views of life.   In 1811, they were
married according to Quaker rites.   Then began one
of the happiest of wedded lives, — and in spite of
privations, for James Mott always found it difficult to
support his family.

When Lucretia's father died, leaving her mother
with three children to support, the Motts did all they
could to help her.   Lucretia opened a school for the
purpose, and soon afterward her husband's business
ventures prospered, so that he, too, could assist.

Just as their prospects were brightening, however,
there came a severe blow in the death of their only
son.   Lucretia then gave up teaching and spent a
great deal of time in the study of the Bible and of
theology.   She used to read William Penn, Dean

Stanley, and John Stuart Mill with her baby on her knee.

Soon she took her place as a preacher in the Society of Friends, feeling "called," as she tells us, "to a public life of usefulness"; and during the latter part of the year 1818, she accompanied another minister named Sarah Zane to Virginia, for the purpose of holding religious meetings. Here Mrs. Mott came into contact with the question of slavery, and in all her discourses she never failed to urge the doctrine of emancipation. She believed in liberty of the body and liberty of thought; indeed, her belief in liberty may be said to have been the basis of all her sermons.

The Quakers who held slaves freed them as early as 1774. The Society of Friends, to which Mr. and Mrs. Mott belonged, became so interested in the slavery question as to recommend that any goods produced by slave-labor should not be handled by any Quaker in regular standing. Mr. Mott was at that time engaged in a prosperous cotton business, but consistent with his views, he gave up this business, — for a while finding great difficulty in making a living.

In 1833, the Female Anti-Slavery Society was formed in Philadelphia. Mrs. Mott was one of four women who, braving public opinion, gave their voices to the cause of Freedom. She was President of the society during most of its existence; and it was due mainly to her inspiring presence, her courage and activity, and her unfailing dignity, that the society accomplished its great work.

She sheltered fugitive slaves, everywhere befriended the colored people, and traveled from place to place preaching the doctrine of liberty.

Young people of the present time can hardly understand the bitter and fierce opposition encountered by those people who were working to free the slaves. For many years, public feeling on the subject was so intense that many anti-slavery meetings were broken up by acts of violence. Sometimes mobs of men and women stoned the windows of the houses where these meetings were being held, breaking into the assemblage, leaping upon the platform, and shouting so loudly that the speaker's voice was lost in the noise.

In 1838, during a riot in Philadelphia, a mob burned Pennsylvania Hall, and then marched through the streets threatening an attack upon the house of James and Lucretia Mott. Mrs. Mott sent her children out of the house to a place of safety, and she, with her husband and a few friends, sat quietly waiting for the mob.   Before it reached the house, however, the leaders urged the rioters to attack a home for colored orphans in another part of the city, and · so the raid upon the Mott house was given up for that night.

At another time, when the mob was expected, and when Mr. and Mrs. Mott, surrounded by their friends, sat listening to the angry cries of threatening men outside, it happened that in the crowd was a young man friendly to the Mott family.   He cried, "On to the Motts'!" and purposely ran up the wrong street.   The rioters followed him blindly, and the Motts were a second time saved from violence.

Women who had formerly been Mrs. Mott's friends passed her on the street without speaking, and scornful people laughed at her.   Sometimes rough men, carried away by the excitement of the times, surged round her like maniacs, threatening violence, but Mrs. Mott never lost her temper or her composed manner.   In her own story of her life she says, "The misrepresentation, ridicule and abuse heaped upon these reforms do not in the least deter me from my duty."

When the National Anti-Slavery Society was formed, Mrs. Mott took a prominent part, offering suggestions with "such charm and precision that they were readily assented to." In this work she was associated with Garrison, Whittier, and other noted Abolitionists.

In 1840, Mrs. Mott was sent to London to represent the Abolitionists of the United States at the World's Anti-Slavery Convention, where she met Elizabeth Cady Stanton, also a delegate. They were not permitted to take their places in the Convention, for by a vote taken at their first sitting, that body decided that only men were to be admitted. Aside from this, however, the women were treated with the greatest courtesy. But, though their feelings were supposed to be salved by being given seats of honor in the hall, they felt keenly the humiliation of their position. It was certainly an indignity.

Mrs. Mott had for years been accustomed to speaking in public, people of all denominations coming many miles to hear the great Quaker preacher. Her home had been a refuge for hunted slaves, and all her eloquence was devoted to the cause of their freedom. Without doubt, she was one of the most prominent persons present at this meeting. She, if anyone, should have been allowed to speak in behalf of humanity.

Out of the indignation aroused on this occasion in the minds of Mrs. Mott and Mrs. Stanton, grew the Woman Suffrage Movement. The first Woman's Rights Convention was called in Seneca Falls, New York, July, 1848, the rights of women to the ballot and their equality with man under the law being the subjects discussed.

James Mott approved of his wife's course and assisted her all that he could by presiding at the first meeting. No end of ridicule was heaped upon the women who thus openly claimed equal rights with men, but Mrs. Mott argued her cause so politely and so wittily that her opponents were disarmed. It is a pleasure to know that Lucretia Mott lived to see the slaves freed and to note the change of public opinion toward herself and others who had worked for freedom.

When Mrs. Mott was seventy-five and her husband eighty years of age, they went to Brooklyn to visit their grandchildren. While there, Mr. Mott was taken ill with pneumonia and passed away quietly while his wife was sleeping on the pillow beside him. Colored men bore him to his grave, at their own request, to show their regard for one who had worked so persistently to benefit their race. The Motts'

married life had been one of great happiness, not the
slightest shadow having ever come between them.
One who knew them well said, "Theirs was the most
perfect wedded life to be found on earth."

Mrs. Mott was greatly solaced to know that her
opponents had changed their opinions in respect to
her. During the latter part of her life, it was no
unusual thing for a stranger to stop her in the street
and ask the privilege of shaking hands. Once a
woman in mourning passed quickly by her, whisper-
ing, "God bless you, Lucretia Mott."

Each Christmas Day she visited the Colored Home
in Philadelphia, carrying turkeys and pies and personal gifts to every inmate. She also sent a box
of candy to every conductor and brakeman on the
railroad on which she traveled, saying: "They never
let me lift out my bundles, and they all seem to
know me!" The number of children, both black
and white, named after her, was astonishing.

At the Centennial Anniversary of the Old Pennsylvania Abolition Society, Lucretia Mott was
greeted by the vast audience with cheers and waving
of handkerchiefs and hats. Another ovation occurred
at a July Fourth meeting of the National Woman
Suffrage Association. When she rose to speak some-

one called to her, "Go up into the pulpit!" As she ascended the pulpit steps, all sang, "Nearer, my God, to Thee!"

Mrs. Mott lived twelve years after her husband's death; then she too passed away, on November 11, 1880, at the age of eighty-seven.

All women have cause to remember her with affection, for she braved public opinion to secure recognition for them.

MARY LYON

MARY LYON

(1797 – 1849)

"Human kind is but one family. The education of its youth should be equal and universal."

—Frances Wright D'Arusmont

To-day if a girl wishes to obtain an education equal to that of a man, the doors of many colleges and other institutions of learning are open to her. It is not so many years ago that this was not the case. Most people, then, thought that girls had no need for a knowledge of the higher branches, and it is largely owing to Mary Lyon that the young women of to-day have such splendid advantages for education.

Born in Buckland, in Western Massachusetts, February 28, 1797, Mary began life, poor and obscure. She was the fifth of a family of seven children, and her early life was one of hard work and of meager opportunity.

Yet it was not unhappy. Her mountain home was well kept, and her parents governed entirely by kindness, insisting upon gentle words, pleasant looks and thoughtfulness for others, on the part of all the children. Out of doors all was beautiful. The mountains, the rocks and streams, the fine trees which surrounded the house, — all gave˘ the child much pleasure. To Mary it seemed as though the peaches and the strawberries raised on their own little farm were larger and more delicious than any others. Her parents had a wonderful faculty for making things grow, and the neighbors said that the plants in Mrs. Lyon's dooryard always bloomed more luxuriantly than any others in the neighborhood.

When Mary was four years old her father died, but her mother, with the help of a hired man, continued the work of the farm and succeeded in supporting her family. Mary, as she grew up, did much of the housework and the spinning. In those days, nearly every family spun the thread to weave the cloth for their own garments, and by the time she was twelve years old, Mary had become expert at this work.

At the age of seven, Mary walked two miles to school. She delighted in her studies and made such rapid progress that visitors to the school were astonished. Finally, the district school moved still farther away, and then Mary went to Ashfield to study,

living there during school months and doing housework to pay for her board.

Every spare moment was spent over her books
and, when she was twelve years old, Mary Lyon
determined to become a teacher. None of the other
girls in the school had any definite purpose as to the
future. The boys planned to become carpenters,
farmers, teachers, lawyers, or ministers, but girls
were supposed to become wives, mothers and house-
keepers, for which offices no special training was
thought necessary. Since that time, fortunately
for the race, public opinion has changed in this respect; to-day, everybody knows that in order to
manage a household well, to rear children, and to
make a happy home, girls need to have a great deal
of knowledge.

When Mary Lyon announced her intention of being
a teacher, the community was astonished, not to say
shocked. It was predicted that she would fail.
Men, not women, were meant for the teaching profession! Mary's proficiency in her studies, however,
could not be denied. Early and late she pored over
her books; in four days, to the amazement of her
teacher, she learned all of Alexander's Grammar and
recited it perfectly. When she was thirteen, her

mother married again and went to live in Ohio, but Mary remained on the farm and kept house for her only brother. He paid her one dollar a week — a large sum for a girl to earn in the year 1810.

For a while it looked as though her high ambitions would never be realized, but the brave girl did not know the word despair. She studied all she could and read every book she could lay her hands upon. After five years spent in this way her brother married and went away, leaving his sister free to do as she pleased.

Thus thrown entirely upon her own resources, Mary began her career as a teacher in Shelburne Falls. Seventy-five cents a week and board made up her munificent salary. By dint of spinning and weaving for some of the neighbors, she earned a little more. Luckily, she did not care for fine clothes or trinkets, so that at the age of twenty she had saved enough money to enable **her** to spend a term at Sanderson Academy at Ashfield. This was her great opportunity and she improved it well, making a real sensation in the school by her brilliancy. They say that when Mary Lyon stood up to recite, her classmates laid aside their tasks to listen to her.

The term over, Mary planned to go back to teaching, for she had no money to continue her studies. It so happened that some of the trustees of the Academy, hearing of her unusual scholarship, offered her another term, tuition free. Mary thankfully accepted this favor, and doubtless, had wonderful dreams of the use she might make of all her knowledge when she should get it. But, first, she must plan some way to pay her board while studying. Among her possessions were some bedding, some table linen, and a few other household articles. These she succeeded in exchanging at a boarding house for a room and a seat at table. Her companions in the boarding house told of her that she slept but four hours, spending all the remainder of her time at her books.

But though she had now reached a point in scholarship where she could easily hold a position as teacher, Mary Lyon by no means considered her education completed. All her vacations were spent in the study of some branch in which she found herself deficient. She spent some time in the family of the Reverend Edward Hitchcock, afterward President of Amherst College, with whom she studied natural science, at the same time taking lessons in drawing and painting from his wife.

In 1821, at the age of twenty-four, Mary had saved

enough money to enable her to enter the school of Reverend Joseph Emerson at Byfield. Her friends were strongly opposed to her going, telling her that she knew enough already; that, as she would never be a minister, it was unnecessary for her to study more. But Mary had other ideas, and could not be diverted from her purpose.

Mr. Emerson was a broad-minded man of very advanced notions for his day and generation. He actually believed that women could understand philosophical subjects as well as men and that, if their minds demanded good solid food, they ought to have it! His wife was a woman of much ability, and together they discussed questions of science and religion with their pupils.

It was undoubtedly these discussions that turned Mary Lyon's mind and thoughts to spiritual things. Heretofore, she had been so absorbed in her passion for general knowledge that the matter of religion had never touched her. Suddenly the fact burst upon her that all things in this life were useless and unsatisfying, except as they were used in helping humanity. From this time on, her work of teaching seemed little short of inspired.

When, later, an assistant was wanted at Sanderson

Academy, notwithstanding the opposition of many who believed that a man should fill the place, Mary Lyon was selected for the position. Before long one of her former teachers, Miss F. P. Grant, sent for her to fill a higher position at Derry, New Hampshire. Mary delayed going in order to take some lessons in chemistry from Professor Eaton of Amherst.

The school in Derry numbered ninety pupils. It was held only during the summer months, and during the winter Mary again taught at Ashfield and Bucklands. She charged twenty-five cents a week for tuition, the scholars boarding with families in the vicinity, at the rate of $1.25 weekly. Meanwhile Miss Grant, who had removed to Ipswich, induced Miss Lyon to join her there. Together they conducted the Ipswich Academy, and together they worked out their ideas of what a school should be.

During these years of teaching, Mary Lyon's heart had been full of sympathy for girls who desired an education but could not obtain it. There were no scholarships offered in those days and the doors of men's colleges were closed to women. At Ipswich, Mary found it impossible to conduct a good school on the income derived from the fees of the pupils. So she tried to interest wealthy men, ministers, and college presidents in her plan of forming a high-grade school or college for women, asking those who were able, to donate a sum of money for the purpose.

Most of these men refused to aid her in the project, repeating the old story that "girls had no need for a knowledge of science or the classics; that, in fact, they were unfitted for studying advanced branches." Miss Lyon held a quite different view, and stuck to her purpose through every discouragement.

Yet, sometimes even brave Mary Lyon had moments of despondency, when she would weep bitterly over her failure to interest others in her plans. But the idea of giving up the work never crossed her mind. She often said to her pupils, "If you feel depressed, think of others, not of yourself!"

About this time she refused a good offer of marriage, saying that her life was devoted to one purpose and that she must give herself entirely to her work. She prayed, and begged her mother to pray, for success. Over and over again she would say: "Commit thy way unto the Lord. He will keep thee. Women *must* be educated. They *must* be!"

At last her faith turned to a faint hope. People began to be interested, and she now gave all her time to the work of soliciting funds. It was her desire to raise the first thousand dollars from women, and this she succeeded in doing in two months' time. Dr. Hitchcock, always her staunch friend, aided her with his support and approval, and one by one broadminded, noble men lent their assistance, until the Female Seminary was an assured thing.

On October 3, 1836, the corner stone of Mount Holyoke Seminary was laid at South Hadley, Massachusetts. Mary Lyon in writing to a friend of the occasion said: "I have indeed lived to see the time when a body of gentlemen has ventured to lay the corner stone of an edifice, which will cost $15,000 and which will be an institution for the education of females. This will be an era in female education."

In about one year the Seminary was opened to pupils. Since its advantages were intended chiefly to benefit poor girls, the charges were placed at the low figure of sixty dollars a year for board and tuition. There were accommodations for eighty pupils, but one hundred and sixteen attended the first year!

In order to lessen expenses, as well as to insure good health and to teach domestic science, all the household work was done by the pupils. Moreover, if it could be shown that the graduates of the Seminary had acquired a knowledge of household matters together with their classical and scientific studies, the prejudice which existed against education for girls might be lessened.

Miss Lyon received a salary of two hundred dollars a year, and her teachers received from one hundred to one hundred and fifty dollars each. Catherine Beecher once took Mary Lyon to task for the small salaries paid her teachers. Miss Lyon replied, "In a list of motives for teaching, I should first place the great motive, 'Love thy neighbor as thyself'." She aimed to employ only such teachers as would work as she did — for the benefit of humanity. Her own best reward was the love which her pupils manifested for her, and the respect with which they treated her.

She never had any trouble with discipline because she never required anything of the students but compliance with the ordinary rules of lady-like behavior, consideration for others, and attention to their studies. They were expected to do right, or to go away. The fact is that none but earnest workers sought to enter Mount Holyoke.

After twelve years as Principal of Mount Holyoke Seminary, Miss Lyon died, March 5, 1849, and was buried in the Seminary grounds. Over her grave is a beautiful monument of white Italian marble bearing the memorable sentence she uttered when giving her last instruction to her scholars:

"There is nothing in the world I fear, but that I shall not know all my duty or shall fail to do it!"

To her was due one of the greatest revolutions in the history of our country. She reversed the prevailing opinion of the men of that time regarding female education, and was the grand pioneer in a movement which has gone steadily forward ever since.

To-day the property of Mount Holyoke is worth $3,000,000. Thousands of girls have been educated there, many of whom have become missionaries and teachers. Many others have married, their education enabling them to be better wives and mothers, and to do their full duty in any station in life to which they may be called.

DOROTHEA DIX

DOROTHEA DIX

(1802 – 1887)

"Great women belong to history and to self-sacrifice."
—*Leigh Hunt*

Dorothea Dix has been called "the most useful and distinguished woman America has yet produced." Let us follow the events of her life and decide for ourselves whether this statement is true.

Dorothea Lynde Dix was born April 4, 1802, at Hampden, Maine. Her father, Joseph Dix, was a man of unstable character and of a most singular mental make-up. In fact, he was regarded as almost insane on religious questions. He wandered about from place to place writing and publishing tracts, spending in this way the little money he had, without regard to the needs of his family. His wife and children were required to assist in the stitching and pasting of the tracts, a tiresome work which brought them no return.

At twelve years of age Dorothea rebelled against this labor. She wished to attend school, but there was little chance for her to study while she lived with her father.   So she ran away from Worcester, where the family then lived, and went to Boston, the home of her grandmother, Mrs. Dorothea Lynde Dix.

Mrs. Dix received the girl as kindly as her nature would permit.   But she was a stern woman, with very strict ideas of training children, and every piece of work done for her had to be perfectly performed or severe punishment followed.

Once, when little Dorothea had failed to accomplish a task as well as her grandmother thought she should, she was compelled to spend a whole week alone without speaking to anyone.   This sounds cruel, but Dorothea's grandmother wished to make the child careful and painstaking.

Poor little Dorothea!   She said in after years that she "never knew childhood."   But she submitted to her grandmother's sternness rather than return to her father and the wandering, useless life he led. She had always in mind the day when she would be able to support herself and help her younger brothers. So she studied diligently, and being clever, made great progress.   When she was fourteen, she returned to Worcester, where she opened a small school for young children.   In order to look old enough for a teacher, she lengthened the skirts of her dresses and arranged her hair grown-woman fashion.

The school succeeded, for Dorothea, though always kind and gentle, was a strict disciplinarian. The year following, she returned to Boston and studied to fit herself for more advanced work in teaching. In 1821, when she was nineteen years of age, she opened a day and boarding school in that city, in a house belonging to her grandmother. Here she received pupils from the best families in Boston and the neighboring towns, and was able to send for her brothers and educate them, while supporting herself. Dorothea's sympathies, meanwhile, were drawn to the poor children about her, who had no means of obtaining an education because their parents could not afford to pay the tuition. She put the matter before her austere grandmother, and begged for the use of a loft over the stable for a school room for these children. The little "barn school" was the beginning of a movement that grew, and later resulted in the Warren Street Chapel.

You may imagine how happy Dorothea Dix was now, — to be self-supporting and to be helping others to become so! She managed the two schools, had the care of her two brothers, and took entire charge of her grandmother's home. For Mrs. Dix had learned to admire and trust the granddaughter whom she had once found so careless.

This amount of work would completely fill the lives of most people, yet Dorothea found time to prepare a text-book upon *Common Things.* Sixty editions of the book were printed and sold. It was followed by two others: *Hymns for Children* and *Evening Hours.*

In order to do all this work, she arose early and sat up late into the night. Naturally her health failed under such a strain. After six years she gave up her schools, and took a position as governess in a family living at Portsmouth, Rhode Island. Here she lived much in the open air, and her great desire for universal knowledge led her to make a special study of botany and marine life.

Her health failing again, she visited Philadelphia, and then went South as far as Alexandria, Virginia, writing short stories the while to support herself. The winter of 1830 she spent in the West Indies with the family of Dr. Channing. There she at last regained her health.

The following spring, Miss Dix returned to Boston, and reopened her school in the old Dix homestead.

Pupils flocked to her, and for five years the work flourished. Her influence over her pupils was wonderful. They thought her very beautiful, as indeed she was. Mrs. Livermore writes of her: "Miss Dix was slight and delicate in appearance. She must have been beautiful in her youth and was still very sweet looking, with a soft voice, graceful figure and winning manners."

In 1836, ill health obliged her to close her school once more. This time she went to England. Though only thirty-four, she had saved enough money to enable her to live in comfort without labor. Shortly after, her grandmother died, leaving her enough to carry out the plans for helping others, which had become a part of her life. She then returned from England and made her home in Washington.

In 1841, however, we find her again in Boston and at this time her real life-work began. It happened that a minister well known to Miss Dix had charge of a Sunday school in the East Cambridge jail. He needed a teacher to take charge of a class of twenty women, and asked Miss Dix if she could tell him of any suitable person.

Miss Dix thought the matter over and then said, "I will take the class myself!"

Her friends objected because of her frail health, but having once arrived at a decision, Dorothea Dix never changed her mind. As one of her pupils said, "Fixed as fate, we considered her!"

The following Sunday, after the session was over, she went into the jail and talked with many of the prisoners. It seemed that they had many righteous grievances, one being that no heat of any kind was provided for their cells.

When Miss Dix asked the keeper of the jail to heat the rooms, he replied that the prisoners did not need heat, and that besides, stoves would be unsafe. Though she begged him to do something to make the cells more comfortable, he refused. She then brought the case before the Court in East Cambridge. The Court granted her request and heat was furnished the prisoners.

In the East Cambridge jail she saw many things too horrible to believe. The cells were dirty, the inmates crowded together in poorly ventilated quarters, the sane and insane often being placed in the same room. These conditions, and others too sad to mention, she made public through the newspapers and the pulpits. But she did not stop at this. Every jail and almshouse in Massachusetts was visited by her;

she must see for herself how the unfortunate inmates were treated. For two years she traveled about, visiting these institutions and taking notes. Then she prepared her famous Memorial to the Legislature.

In this Memorial Miss Dix said: "I proceed, gentlemen, briefly to call your attention to the present state of insane persons within this Commonwealth, in cages, closets, cellars, stalls, pens, chained and naked, beaten with rods and lashed into obedience." Proofs were offered for all facts stated.

The Memorial was presented by Dr. S. G. Howe, husband of Julia Ward Howe. Dr. Howe was then a member of the Legislature. The conditions thus made public shocked the entire community, so that, after much discussion, a bill was passed enlarging the asylum at Worcester. A small beginning, yet the grand work of reform was started, and Miss Dix was grateful.

She then turned her attention to other States, visiting the jails, almshouses, and insane asylums as far west as Illinois and as far south as Louisiana. In Rhode Island she found the insane shockingly treated.

At that time there lived in Providence a very rich man named Butler. He had never been known to give anything to help the unfortunate, but Miss Dix decided to appeal to him.   People smiled when they heard that she intended to call upon Mr. Butler and ask him for money.

During the call, he talked of everything except the subject nearest Miss Dix's heart, "talking against time," as they say, to prevent her from putting the vital question.   At length she said in a quiet but forceful manner:

"*Mr. Butler, I wish you to hear what I have to say. I bring before you certain facts involving terrible suffering to your fellow creatures, suffering you can relieve.*"

She then told him what she had seen.

Mr. Butler heard her story to the end without interruption.   Then he said,

"What do you want me to do?"

"I want you to give $50,000 to enlarge the insane hospital in this city!"

"Madam, I'll do it!" was the reply.

After three years of this sort of work, Miss Dix became an expert on the question of how an insane asylum should be built and managed.   In New Jersey, she succeeded after much hard work in securing the passage of a bill establishing the New Jersey State

Lunatic Asylum, and the money necessary to build it. This building was a model for the times.

For twelve years she went up and down through the United States in the interests of the suffering insane, securing the enlargement of three asylums and the building of thirteen.

In 1850, Miss Dix secured the passage of a bill giving twelve million acres of public lands for the benefit of the poor insane, the deaf and dumb, and the blind. Applause went up all over the country, yet, strange to say, after the passage of the bill by both Houses, President Franklin Pierce vetoed it!

This was a severe blow to Miss Dix and she again went to Europe for a rest. But rest she could not. All the large European cities had abuses of this kind to be corrected, and she must work to help them.

A most interesting story is told of her encounter with Pope Pius IX. In vain had she tried to get authority in Rome to enable her to do something to improve the horrible Italian prisons. She had even tried, but vainly, to get audience with the Pope. One day she saw his carriage, *stopped it*, and addressed him, willy-nilly, in *Latin*, as she knew no Italian. Her enterprise appears to have impressed the Pope favorably, for he gave her everything she asked for. In her

own country, again, she extended her labors to the
Western States. Then the breaking out of the Civil
War rendered such labors useless.

But now there were the soldiers to help! Her
active interest in them came about in the following
way:

Shortly after April, 1861, she happened to be passing through Baltimore when the Sixth Regiment of
Massachusetts, on its way to Washington, was
stoned by a vast mob, several men being killed.
At once Miss Dix knew what to do. She took the
first train she could get for Washington, and reported
at the War Department for free service in the hospitals, where through Secretary Simon Cameron, she
immediately received the appointment as "Superin-
tendent of Women Nurses." Here, truly, was an
enormous piece of work for her.

Among her duties were the selection and assign-
ment of women nurses; the superintendence of the
thousands of women already serving; the seeing
that supplies were fairly distributed; and looking
after the proper care of wounded soldiers. Her remarkable executive ability soon brought order and
system out of confusion. It is said that she accepted
no women who were under thirty years of age, and

demanded that they be plain in dress and without beauty. Good health and good moral character were also, of course, requirements.

Many of the surgeons and nurses disliked her. They said she was severe, that she would not listen to any advice nor take any suggestions. The real cause of her unpopularity, however, was that she demanded of all about her entire unselfishness and strict devotion to work. Very severe was she with careless nurses or rough surgeons.

Two houses were rented by her to hold the supplies sent to her care, and still other houses were rented for convalescent soldiers or nurses who needed rest. She employed two secretaries, owned ambulances and kept them busy, printed and distributed circulars, settled disputes in matters which concerned her nurses, took long journeys when necessary, and paid from her own private purse many expenses incurred. Everything she possessed — fortune, time, strength — she gave to her country in its time of need.

During the four years of the War, Miss Dix never took a holiday. Often she had to be reminded of her meals, so interested was she in the work. At the close of the War, when the Hon. Edwin M. Stanton, then Secretary of War, asked her how the nation could best thank her for her services, she answered, "I would like a flag."

Two beautiful flags were given to her with a suitable inscription. These flags she bequeathed to Harvard College, and they now hang over the doors of Memorial Hall.

The War over, Miss Dix again took up her work for the insane and for fifteen years more devoted herself to their welfare.

In 1881, at the age of seventy-nine, she retired to the hospital she had been the means of building at Trenton, New Jersey, and here she was tenderly cared for until her death in 1887.

MARGARET FULLER D'OSSOLI

MARGARET FULLER D'OSSOLI

(1810 – 1850)

"I have always said it: Nature meant to make woman its masterpiece."

— *Gotthold Ephraim Lessing*

Margaret Fuller was born in Cambridgeport, Massachusetts, May 23, 1810. Her parents were people of great culture and refinement, and devotedly attached to each other. Margaret wrote years after her father's death:

"His love for my mother was the green spot on which he stood apart from the commonplaces of a mere bread-winning existence. She was one of those fair, flowerlike natures, which sometimes spring up even beside the most dusty highways of life. Of all persons whom I have known, she had in her most of the angelic."

It was not surprising therefore that Margaret should have inherited a beautiful nature and a fine mind. She became the idol of her father, who was fifty years in advance of his neighbors in his ideas of bringing up

75

girls. Mr. Fuller believed that his daughter should have as good an education as his boys! But since there were no girls' colleges, and the boys' colleges were closed to them, he was obliged to teach Margaret himself.

At six years of age this clever child began to read Latin. Once, when she was eight, her father found her so absorbed in *Romeo and Juliet* that she did not hear him when he spoke to her. It is probable that much of Margaret's later ill-health was the result of the severe mental work demanded of her in childhood by her father.

Mr. Fuller was certainly very ambitious that Margaret should excel in her studies. Often she remained up until late at night reciting to him, not knowing that she was working beyond her strength.

She describes her life at the age of fifteen in the following manner:

"I rise a little before five, walk an hour, and then practice on the piano until seven, when we breakfast. Next, I read French till eight; then two or three lectures in Brown's Philosophy. About half past nine, I go to Mr. Perkins's School and study Greek till twelve, when, the school being dismissed, I recite, go home, and practice again till dinner at two. Then when I can, I read two hours in Italian."

Though frail in body and plain in looks, this young girl grew to be a fascinating and attractive woman. Men and women of prominence fell under the influence of her charms. At seventeen, her unusual intellectual qualities gained her the friendship of Rev. James Freeman Clark; and later she became a valued friend of the Emerson family.

At the age of twenty-three, Margaret taught in the famous school of Mr. Alcott in Boston. Through working with this great educator, she met most of the gifted men and women of the time. Elizabeth Peabody, another remarkable woman, to whom we are indebted for bringing Froebel and the Kindergarten into notice in the United States, became Margaret's friend, and together these two labored to revive intellectual thought among women.

When Mr. Alcott ceased teaching, Margaret became Principal of a school in Providence, Rhode Island. But longing to become better educated herself, she resigned from her position to give private lessons in the higher branches, meanwhile studying languages. So great were her acquisitive powers that before long she had a good teaching knowledge of Latin, Greek, German, French, and Italian.

Her greatest gift was her ability to entertain people

by conversing with them.   Deeply interested in the welfare of women, her talent for talking led her to open a "School of Conversation."   A large number of intelligent, educated women met in the home of Miss Elizabeth Peabody where, led by Margaret Fuller, they discussed important books and philosophical subjects.   Her idea was to induce women to do something worth while with their knowledge.

These *Conversations* were ridiculed by the community at large, yet they were continued successfully for five years, and attracted many serious and intellectual women who felt the need of mental activity.   At last the *Conversations* became an old story, and Margaret looked about for other occupation.   One came to her in the form of an editorial position on the New York Tribune offered her by Horace Greeley, the. editor-in-chief.   She used her pen, also, for the benefit of the people, writing editorials to influence the rich to help the poor, the unjust to become just.   She also translated books from foreign languages, and kept a journal which was published after her death.

In 1847, Miss Fuller went to Rome to live, and while there met a handsome young Italian named Giovanni Angelo, the Marchese d'Ossoli.   This gentleman had been discarded by his family for his part in a political movement led by Mazzini for the independence of Italy. His troubles attracted Margaret to him, they became attached to each other, and finally married.

It was necessary, however, to keep the marriage a secret, Margaret being a Protestant. During the siege of Rome by the French army in 1849, Margaret, still known as Miss Fuller, took an active part in hospital work, spending the greater part of her time in nursing the sick and wounded.

The Marchese d'Ossoli, had charge of the battery on Pincian Hill, the most exposed of all positions. Such great fear was felt for the men stationed there that Margaret summoned Mr. Cass, the American minister at Rome, and gave him certain letters and papers. He was astonished to learn from these that she was married to d'Ossoli, and that the package contained the certificate of their marriage and that of the birth and baptism of their child; also that she intended to go to the Pincian Hill, remain with her husband and die with him if necessary.

Mr. Cass willingly took charge of these papers, and watched the Marchese and Margaret walk away together as if on a pleasant stroll. They survived the night, however, and next morning the French army entered Rome. Soon after, the Marchese and Marchesa with their child left Rome for Florence, to sail for America as soon as possible.

It is recorded that both dreaded the voyage, as d'Ossoli had been told by a fortune-teller to avoid the sea, and Margaret had a strong presentiment of disaster.

They sailed May 5, 1850, and from the first the voyage was a bad one. The captain died of small-pox and had to be buried at sea. Then wind-storms delayed them; and when little Angelo was taken ill with small-pox, the agony of the parents may be imagined. The child recovered, but on July 19, during a terrific gale, the vessel was wrecked off Fire Island, and Margaret, her husband, and her child were lost.

A trunk containing papers and manuscripts belonging to Margaret was picked up, and in this way her relatives and friends came to know the true history of her life abroad.

HARRIET BEECHER STOWE

HARRIET BEECHER STOWE

(1811 – 1896)

"Give her of the fruit of her hands and let her own works praise her at the gates."

—*Solomon*

Few women's names have made so vivid a mark upon the history of our country as that of Harriet Beecher Stowe, the author of Uncle Tom's Cabin.

On June 14, 1811, in the little town of Litchfield, Connecticut, Harriet first saw the light of day. She was the seventh child, the eldest being but eleven years of age. Just two years after Harriet was born came a little brother, Henry Ward, who became the renowned pastor of Plymouth Church, Brooklyn.

Harriet's father, the Reverend Lyman Beecher, was a man of marked ability, and her mother, Roxanna Beecher, was a woman whose beautiful life has been a help to many. The family was a large one to be supported on a salary of five hundred dollars a year, and in order to assist, Roxanna Beecher started a select school, where she taught French, drawing, painting and embroidery, as well as the higher English branches.

A great grief came to little Harriet, when she was between three and four, in the death of her mother. Certain things in connection with this event, as the funeral, the mourning dresses, and the walk to the burial ground; never left her memory. Her little mind was confused by being told that her mother had gone to heaven, when Harriet had with her own eyes seen her laid in the ground. Her brother Henry suffered likewise from this confusion of thought. He was found one day in the garden digging diligently. When his elder sister Catherine asked him what he was doing, he answered: "I'm going to heaven to find mamma!"

When Harriet was six, her father married again. At first the little girl, who had loved her own mother so dearly, felt very sad about this; but she afterward learned to love and respect her new mother.

Harriet had a remarkable memory. At seven she had memorized twenty-seven hymns and two long chapters in the Bible. She read fluently, and continually searched her father's library for books which might interest her. Very few did she find there, however. Most of the titles filled her childish soul with awe, and she longed for the time when she could understand and enjoy such works as Bonnett's *Inquiries*, Bell's *Sermons*, and Bogue's *Essays*.

One day good luck befell her. In the bottom of a barrel of old sermons she came upon a well-worn volume of *The Arabian Nights*. Imagine her joy! A world of enchantment opened to her. When *Ivanhoe* fell in her way, she and her brother George read it through, together, seven times.

It was in the school of Mr. John P. Brace that Harriet discovered her taste for writing. Her compositions were remarkable for their cleverness; when one of them was read at the entertainment at the close of the year, Harriet's cup of joy was full to the brim.

About this time Harriet's elder sister, Catherine, opened a school in Hartford. The circumstances which led her to do so were very sad. Catherine, who was remarkably gifted, had been engaged to Professor Fisher of Yale, a brilliant and promising young man. These young people expected to be married on the return of the Professor from a European trip. But the vessel on which he sailed was wrecked, and he never came back.

This almost prostrated Catherine, but her strong

nature rose to meet the blow. She determined to devote her life to the work of helping girls. After hard work she raised several thousands of dollars and built the Hartford Female Seminary, where girls studied subjects heretofore taught only in boys' colleges, and received an éducation more on an equality with that given to boys.

People of that time wondered what use girls would make of Latin and philosophy, but Miss Beecher's able management of the school and her womanly and scholarly attainments so filled them with admiration that they gladly put their daughters in her charge. Here also entered twelve year old Harriet, not only as a pupil, but a pupil teacher, that she might help her father in paying the expenses of his large family. The experience of Harriet in this school was of much use in after life. She had to master problems without any assistance from others, and in doing this, she became self-reliant.

About ten years after this, her father was called to become President of Lane Theological Seminary at Cincinnati, Ohio. Catherine and Harriet felt bound to go with him, to help him in the new field of work. The journey, made by stage-coach across the mountains, was very tiresome. They settled in

Walnut Hills, a suburb of Cincinnati, where the sisters opened another school.

In 1836, Harriet married Calvin E. Stowe, professor of Biblical Criticism and Oriental Literature in the Lane Seminary. Mr. Stowe, together with other intelligent men in Ohio at that time, was much interested in the advancement of education in the common schools. In order to study the question and to purchase books for the Lane Seminary, Mr. Stowe was sent abroad. This happened shortly after his marriage.

During his absence Harriet lived in Cincinnati with her father and brother, writing short stories and essays for publication and assisting her brother, Henry Ward, who was then editing a small daily paper.

The question of slavery had become an exciting topic in Cincinnati. Being near the borderland of Kentucky, a slave state, this city naturally became the center of heated discussions. Many slaves who escaped sought refuge in Cincinnati, and people who were friendly to their cause assisted them to reach Canada, where they were safe from capture by their so called masters.

Among the students of Lane Seminary were both Northerners and Southerners, and many fierce debates as to the rights and wrongs of slavery were carried on in that institution. The feeling was very intense and excitement ran high. Dr. Bailey, an editor who attempted to carry on in his newspaper a fair discussion of the slavery question, had his presses broken and thrown into the river.

Mrs. Stowe took into her family, as servant, a colored girl from Kentucky. Though by the laws of Ohio this girl was free, having been brought into the state by her mistress and left there, yet it was rumored that some one had come to the city from over the border hunting for her, with the intention of taking her back into slavery. Mrs. Stowe and Henry Ward Beecher drove the poor girl by night twelve miles into the country and left her with an old friend until such time as the search for her should be given up. This incident served Mrs. Stowe as the basis of her description in *Uncle Tom's Cabin* of Eliza's escape from Tom Loker and Marks.

Houses of free colored people were burned and even Lane Seminary stood in danger from the mob. Mr. Stowe and his family slept with firearms at hand ready to defend themselves if necessary. When the trustees of the college forbade all discussion of the question of slavery, nearly all the students left the institution.

Then Mrs. Stowe opened her house to colored children and taught them. One boy in her school was claimed by a master in Kentucky, arrested and put up at auction. Mrs. Stowe raised sufficient money to buy him and gave it to his distracted mother, who thus saved him. Heart-rending incidents like this were continually brought to the attention of the Stowe family, until at last they felt unable to endure the situation. They decided to come North where Mr. Stowe accepted a position in Bowdoin College, Maine.

Very poor was the Stowe family in those days. Mrs. Stowe earned a little now and then, by her writings, and from a few boarders. She had now apparently all she could do, with a family of young children whom she herself taught, with her writing, and with caring for the strangers in the house; but even so, she could never get out of her mind those wretched creatures, her brothers and sisters, who were being bought and sold. What could she do for them?

The most frequent topic of conversation everywhere was the proposed law called The Fugitive Slave Act. This law would give the slave-holders of the South the right to bring back into slavery any colored person claimed as a slave, and also commanded the people of the North to assist in the business of pursuit. Public feeling grew more and more heated, but the law was passed. After its passage many pitiable scenes occurred. The Stowe and Beecher families received frequent letters telling of shocking incidents. Families were broken up, children sold and sent far from their parents, while many slaves who ran away perished from cold and hunger.

One day Mrs. Stowe received a letter from her sister-in-law, Mrs. Edward Beecher, which she read to her family. When she came to this passage: *Now, Hattie, if I could use a pen as you can, I would write something that would make the whole nation feel what an accursed thing slavery is,* Mrs. Stowe stood up, an expression upon her face which those who saw it never forgot.

What she said, however, was simply, "I *will* write something! I will, if I live!"

Some months after this Mrs. Stowe was seated at communion in the college church at Brunswick, when the scene of the death of Uncle Tom passed through her mind as clearly as in a vision. She hastened home, wrote out the chapter on his death, as it now stands, and then read it to her assembled family. Her two sons aged eleven and twelve years burst out crying, saying, "Oh, mamma! Slavery is the most cruel thing in the world!"

When two or three more chapters were ready, she offered it for publication to Dr. Bailey, then in Washington, and *Uncle Tom's Cabin* was first published as a serial in his paper *The National Era*. For it Mrs. Stowe received three hundred dollars.

When completed, it was published by Jewett of Boston, in March, 1852, meeting with instant success. In ten days ten thousand copies were sold. Thirty different editions appeared in London in six months, and it was translated into twenty foreign languages. It was dramatized, and several theaters were playing it at one time. In less than a year over three hundred thousand copies were sold.

Mrs. Stowe "woke up to find herself famous," — not to say wealthy. Letters of congratulation poured in upon her from all parts of the world. Queen Victoria and Prince Albert sent hearty thanks. Charles Dickens wrote, "Your book is worthy of any head and any heart that ever inspired a book." Charles Kingsley wrote, "It is perfect!"

The poet Whittier wrote to Garrison, "What a glorious work Harriet Beecher Stowe has wrought!

Thanks for the Fugitive Slave Law!   Better would
it be for slavery if that law had never been enacted,
for it gave occasion for *Uncle Tom's Cabin!*"

Longfellow also wrote in praise of the book, and
letters were received from most of the noted men
who opposed slavery.

The possibility of making money by the publication
of this book was quite remote from Mrs. Stowe's dis-
interested mind.   As she wrote in a letter to a friend:
"Having been poor all my life, and expecting to be
poor for the rest of it, the idea of making money by a
book which I wrote just because I could not help it,
never occurred to me."   But from this time forth
she was to be free from the anxieties of poverty.
As the first payment of three months' sale, Mrs.
Stowe received ten thousand dollars.

The following year Professor and Mrs. Stowe went
to Great Britain, having been urgently invited to
visit in many Scotch and English houses.   Even in
foreign lands, Mrs. Stowe found herself known and
loved.   Crowds greeted her in Liverpool, Glasgow,
Edinburgh and London.   Children ran ahead of her
carriage, throwing flowers to her, and officials of the
Anti-Slavery Societies met her and offered hospitality.

A national penny offering, turned into a thousand golden sovereigns, was presented to her on a magnificent silver salver for the advancement of the cause for which she had written. This offering came from all classes of people.

A personal gift which Mrs. Stowe valued highly was a superb gold bracelet presented by the beautiful Duchess of Sutherland who entertained her at Stafford House. It was made in the form of a slave's shackle and bore the inscription, "We trust it is a memorial of a chain that is soon to be broken." On two of the links were already inscribed the dates of the abolition of slave trade and of slavery in the English territories. Years afterward, on the clasp of the bracelet, Mrs. Stowe had engraved the date of the Constitutional Amendment abolishing slavery in the United States.

Upon Mrs. Stowe's return from her visit to Europe in the autumn of 1853, she became very active in public affairs. She supported anti-slavery lectures, established schools for the colored people, assisted in buying ill-treated slaves and setting them free, and arranged public meetings for the advancement of anti-slavery opinions, using the money which had been given to her in England to support the work.

In addition, she kept up a correspondence with influential men and women on the subject of the abolition of slavery.

The books she wrote after this were *Sunny Memories of Foreign Lands; Dred,* a great anti-slavery story; *The Minister's Wooing; Agnes of Sorrento; The Pearl of Orr's Island;* and *Old Town Folks.*   All have been widely read, but *Uncle Tom's Cabin,* though lacking in literary form and finish, written as it was at white heat and with no thought of anything but its object, remains her greatest work.   It made the enforcement of the Fugitive Slave Law impossible, by making people see slavery in all its inhumanity.

In addition to her books, Mrs. Stowe wrote an appeal to the women of America, in which she set forth the injustice and misery of slavery, begging all thoughtful women to use their influence to have the wicked system abolished.   Here are a few paragraphs:

> What can the women of a country do?   Oh! women of the free states, what did your brave mothers do in the days of the Revolution?   Did not liberty in those days feel the strong impulse of woman's heart?
>
> For the sake, then, of our dear children, for the sake of our common country, for the sake of outraged and struggling liberty throughout the world, let every woman of America now do her duty!

Nobly, indeed, did the women of America respond to her call, for during the Civil War, which was begun before the abolition of slavery was an accomplished fact, the women, though they went not to the war themselves, loyally sent out their fathers, husbands and brothers.   Who shall say these women were not heroic?

After the close of the Civil War, Mrs. Stowe purchased a home in Florida overlooking the St. John's River, where she lived during the winter, going in summer to her old home in Hartford.

On her seventieth birthday, June 14, 1882, her publishers, Messrs. Houghton, Mifflin Company, of Boston, gave a reception for her in the form of a garden party at the beautiful residence of ex-Governor Claflin of Massachusetts in Newtonville, one of Boston's fine suburbs.   Here gathered men and women well known in the literary and artistic world, eager to do honor to the woman whose life had been such an inspiration to others, and whose work of such benefit to mankind.   Mr. Houghton made an address of congratulation and welcome, to which Henry Ward Beecher replied.   Oliver Wendell Holmes spoke, and many poems and letters from noted persons were read.

This was the last public appearance of Mrs. Stowe. Her husband died in August, 1886, and she herself, passed away July 1, 1896, at Hartford, at the age of eighty-four. She was buried in the cemetery of the Theological Seminary at Andover, Massachusetts, next to her husband.

MARIA MITCHELL

MARIA MITCHELL

(1818 – 1889)

"On the cultivation of women's minds depends the wisdom of men."

—Richard Brinsley Sheridan

Maria Mitchell was born on the Island of Nantucket, Massachusetts, August 1, 1818, and to-day if you go there, you may see a monument erected to her memory.

Her ancestors were Quakers who had fled hither from Massachusetts because of religious persecution. Nantucket Island then belonged to New York State, and here these good people were free to worship God as they pleased. Almost all of the inhabitants of the Island belonged to the Society of Friends, from which sect have sprung many of our notable men and women, among them John G. Whittier, "the Quaker Poet," who all his life wore the Quaker garb and spoke the language of that religious society.

The Mitchell family were not very strict; that is, they did not wear the plain clothes of the sect, although they probably used the "thee" and "thou." Maria's mother was a woman of great strength of character. Her father was a kindly gentleman, whose affection for his children was so great that he could refuse them nothing. Often Mrs. Mitchell was obliged to check him, fearing they would be spoiled by his indulgence.

The little girls were brought up to be industrious. They learned to make their own clothes by making those of their dolls, and frequently they made their own dolls, too, the eldest sister painting the faces.

Maria received the first rudiments of her education from her mother and an excellent woman teacher, but not until she entered her father's school, at the age of eleven, did she begin to show marked ability as a student.

Mr. Mitchell was greatly interested in the study of astronomy, and owned a small telescope, which he used to examine the heavens at night. Maria was especially fond of her father's pursuit. She also had a taste for mathematics, without which astronomy as a science cannot be mastered, and she watched, patient and absorbed, when her father would compute distances by means of his scientific instruments.

There was no school in the country where Maria Mitchell could be taught higher mathematics, so she continued to study with her father.

Every fine night the telescope was placed in Mr. Mitchell's back yard, and the neighbors would come in to gaze through it at the moon and the planets. Little Maria was always on hand listening for scraps of information.

In 1831, and while Maria was still a child, there occurred a total eclipse of the sun at Nantucket. With her father, Maria observed this eclipse through a new Dolland telescope which had been recently purchased and, for the first time in her life, counted the seconds of the eclipse. At that time she was studying with Mr. Cyrus Pierce, who took a great interest in her, and who helped her in her mathematics.

At the age of sixteen she left school, becoming for a while an assistant teacher, but she soon gave up teaching to accept the new position of librarian in the Nantucket Atheneum. This post she continued to fill for twenty years. She had much time while acting as a librarian to study her favorite subject, and she used the opportunity to advantage.

Every evening Miss Mitchell spent on the house-top "sweeping" the heavens. One memorable even-

ing, October 1, 1847, she had put on her old clothes
and taken her lantern to the roof as usual. After
gazing through her telescope for a few minutes, she
observed an object which she concluded must be a
comet. Hurriedly she called her father, who also
examined the unusual body in the heavens and agreed
with her that it was a comet.

He immediately announced the discovery to Professor Bond of Cambridge. It was learned afterward
that the same comet had been seen in Rome by an
astronomer on October 3, and in England by another
on October 7, and still later in Germany. To Maria
Mitchell was given the credit of the first discovery, and
she received the gold medal which had been promised by the King of Denmark to the first discoverer
of a telescopic comet. This brought her letters of
congratulation from astronomers in all parts of the
world.

Miss Mitchell had always had a desire to travel
abroad, and as her tastes were simple she soon saved
enough from her small salary to enable her to do so.
During her visits in foreign countries, she met many
eminent scientists, among them Herschel, Airy, Mrs.
Somerville, and Humboldt. The plain Nantucket
lady was perfectly at home in the society of these

distinguished people, whose tastes and occupations were similar to her own. They all opened their observatories for her inspection and their homes for social intercourse.

The Greenwich Observatory especially interested Miss Mitchell. It stands in Greenwich Park, which comprises a group of hills with many beautiful oak trees which are said to date back to the time of Queen Elizabeth. The observatory was then in charge of Sir George Airy, who showed Miss Mitchell all the treasures of the place, among them the instruments used by the great astronomers Halley, Bradley, and Pond. The meridian of Greenwich is the zero point of longitude for the globe, and you can perhaps imagine the pleasure which Miss Mitchell experienced in being on the spot where time is set for the whole world.

Miss Mitchell became Professor of Astronomy and Director of the Observatory at Vassar College, where her work gave the subject a prominence which it has never had in any other woman's college. She was not only a famous astronomer, but a noble, inspiring woman, much interested in the higher education of women and devoting much of her time to advancing this work. Many a young girl can trace the success of her life work to the impulse she received from Maria Mitchell.

At the age of sixty-nine Miss Mitchell's health began to fail and she resigned her position in the College, going to live at her home in Lynn, Massachusetts, where she died June 28, 1889.

. LUCY STONE

LUCY STONE

(1818 – 1893)

" Woman is a creation between men and the angels."
                                        —*Honoré de Balzac*

In the town of West Brookfield, Massachusetts, in 1818, lived a farmer, named Francis Stone, and his wife, a gentle and beautiful woman, whose life was spent in devotion to her husband and in aiding him in his work on the farm. Mrs. Stone worked continuously from early morning until late at night, often milking eight cows after the necessary housework was done. The family consisted of seven children. When, on August 18th, the eighth was born, and Mrs. Stone was told that the new baby was a girl, she said, "Oh, dear! I am sorry it is a girl. A woman's life is so hard!"

It seems as if this little girl, who was called Lucy, must have understood her mother's words, for, as she grew up, she showed very clearly that she intended to try to make life easier for all women. Her childhood was spent in doing useful work about the house and on the farm.   She cooked, swept, dusted, made butter and soap.   She drove the cows, planted seeds, weeded the garden, — in short, was never idle.   But all the time she worked in this way, Lucy was thinking deeply and comparing her life with that of her brother at college.   She pondered deeply over questions like the following:

Why are not girls permitted to earn their living like their brothers?

Why is it that mother works so hard, and father has all the money?

Why are boys given the great benefits of a college education and girls refused it?

She could think of no satisfactory answers.   At last, gathering up her courage, she asked her father to assist her to go to college like her brothers.   Mr. Stone was, both astonished and angry.   He told Lucy that it was enough for her to learn how to read and cipher and write, as her mother did.   But Lucy persisted in her determination to gain an education. She earned a little money by picking berries and gathering chestnuts, and with it she bought some books.   Her mother could not help her, for, though she worked very hard, she had not a penny to bless herself with.   Her husband took all that came in through their joint labors, and spent it as he thought best.

When Lucy had learned enough to fit her for teaching, she got a position in a district school at a salary of one dollar per week. A little later she was earning sixteen dollars a month, and when her brother, who received thirty dollars a month for teaching, became ill, Lucy took his place, receiving sixteen dollars for exactly the same work. The committee said that sixteen dollars was enough for a woman.

Lucy Stone studied for a while at Mt. Holyoke Seminary under Mary Lyon, and also at Wilbraham Academy, and later at Oberlin College, Ohio, which was then the only college in the country willing to admit women, — all the while paying her own tuition fees by means of teaching and doing housework in boarding houses.

When the question of slavery came into prominence, Lucy Stone quickly took her position as a friend of the slave. She taught in a school for colored people, which was established at Oberlin, and her first public speech was made in their behalf. Though severely criticized for her public speaking and obliged to bear unpleasant comment because of it, she never swerved from her idea of what she believed to be right.

Soon she was engaged by the Anti-Slavery Society, in which William Lloyd Garrison and Wendell Phillips were officers, to lecture for their cause, and while doing so, traveled over the greater part of the United States, speaking both for woman suffrage and for the abolition of slavery.

But the rights of woman stood first in the heart of Lucy Stone. As a child, she had seen her mother overruled by a stern husband, who never allowed her an opinion contrary to his will, nor a penny to use without his sanction.

It may have been because of this early object lesson that Lucy Stone made up her mind never to marry; or because she thought that she could carry on her work for the advancement of women better by being entirely free. Nevertheless, she did consent to marry Mr. Henry B. Blackwell, a merchant of Cincinnati, Ohio, who overcame her objections by sharing all her views on suffrage and slavery, and they were married by Rev. Thomas Wentworth Higginson, May 1, 1855.

Before their marriage Mr. Blackwell and Lucy signed a protest which read:

We believe that personal independence and equal human rights can never be forfeited except for crime;

that marriage should be an equal and permanent partnership and so recognized by law.

This protest was the beginning of much serious thought about the rights of man and woman as individuals, and led the way to improved laws. In most states, to-day, a married woman may own her own property and may will a part of it away from her husband, if she wishes to; she may live an individual life, also, and control equally with her husband the education of their children.

Lucy Stone retained her maiden name, never adopting that of her husband. Their married life proved to be remarkably happy, one child, a daughter, being born to them.

Mrs. Stone helped to organize the American Equal Rights Association, which grew into the American Woman Suffrage Association. William Lloyd Garrison, George William Curtis, Colonel Higginson, Julia Ward Howe, and other prominent people joined in the work with her. She served as President of the New England Woman Suffrage Association, and even studied law that she might learn how to correct legal injustice to women. In 1877, Mrs. Stone and Mr. Blackwell went to Colorado to assist in the Woman Suffrage movement in that state. Sixteen years later the constitutional amendment granting the suffrage to woman was carried by popular vote, and women were given "exactly the same rights as men in exercising the elective franchise."

Lucy Stone did not live to see success in Colorado, but she did see school suffrage gained in twenty-two states, and full suffrage in Wyoming. She lived, also, to see many great colleges admit women.

In the summer of 1893, Mrs. Stone was obliged to rest from her labors. A little later she wrote Mrs. Livermore, her devoted friend and co-worker: "I have dropped out, and you will go on without me! Good-by. If we don't meet again, never mind. We shall meet sometime, somewhere; be sure of that."

She passed away in the presence of her husband and her daughter, Alice, on October 18. Her gentleness and sweetness of character had made her beloved by all, and her great work for the advancement of woman in intellectual, social, and political life will never be forgotten.

JULIA WARD HOWE

JULIA WARD HOWE

(1819 – 1910)

" We all are architects of fate,
  Working in these walls of time,
Some with massive deeds and great,
Some with ornaments of rhyme."
— *Henry W. Longfellow*

Julia Ward Howe was born May 27, 1819, in New York City. Her father, Samuel Ward, was a wealthy banker, and her mother a descendant of the Marions of South Carolina, being a grand-niece of General Marion.

Both parents came from families of refined and scholarly tastes, and little Julia directly inherited her love of good books. Her mother died at an early age, leaving six little children, Julia, the fourth, being then only five years old.

Julia, who from babyhood had given promise of superior intellectual attainments, received special attention from her father. Mr. Ward was anxious that she should know the joy which only true knowledge and right living can give. He did not wish her to become merely a fashionable girl with no thought of doing anything in life but amuse herself. Every advantage was given her, therefore, for reading, and the best teachers in music, German, and Italian were selected for her.

Julia well repaid this care. She showed great fondness for books, and at nine years of age was studying Paley's *Moral Philosophy* in a class with girls twice her age. At fourteen, she was an accomplished musician. Her friends thought she should devote her life to music, but she was equally fond of literature. At sixteen she wrote her first poem. Her brother, Samuel Ward, Jr., shared in all her tastes, and together the brother and sister enjoyed the society of the most noted musicians and literary men and women of the day, the poet Longfellow being one of their closest friends.

The death of their beloved father brought a change in the home, and the family went to live with an uncle, Mr. John Ward. Julia continued to spend her time in the cultivation of her mind and in the enjoyment of the fine arts. She excelled in the study of the German language, reading Goethe, Schiller, Swedenborg, Kant, and other great German poets and philosophers, and translating much of their work. She wrote many verses and began to dream of publishing a play.

In Boston, Julia Ward was a welcome addition to the circle of distinguished literary people then living there. She met Margaret Fuller, Horace Mann, Charles Sumner, Ralph Waldo Emerson. All were charmed with the brilliant and intellectual young woman from New York. Dr. Samuel Gridley Howe, a philanthropist and reformer, was one of this delightful group.

Dr. Howe, a graduate of Brown University, was deeply interested in the Greek War for Independence. He went to Greece to offer his services as a surgeon and for the purpose of organizing hospitals, but later took such an active part in the war that he endeared himself to the Greeks for his assistance and sympathy. Contracting a fever, however, he was obliged to leave Greece for a better climate. For some time he traveled abroad, studying and attending lectures.

But to help others was his sole object in life. At that time there were no schools for the blind in the United States. Through Dr. Howe's influence, men of wealth became interested in this matter and helped him to establish such a school. Going again to Europe, to investigate such schools in foreign lands, he was temporarily turned aside from his project by the condition of Poland, oppressed as it then was by Prussia. In consequence of the assistance he gave this unhappy country, he was arrested, and imprisoned for some time.

All the world knows now of Dr. Howe through his kindness to Laura Bridgman, a child, who at the age of two years, and before she had learned to speak, became blind and deaf through a severe illness. When she was about eight, Dr. Howe took her into his home and taught her to read, write, do needlework, and play the piano. His success with Laura was so great that he, later, gave almost his entire energy to work for feeble-minded children and in this accomplished many wonderful results.

Dr. Howe fell in love with Julia Ward. Two such souls could hardly meet and not love each other. Though he was eighteen years older than she, similar tastes and aims naturally united them.

Their marriage took place when Julia was twenty-four years of age. Soon after the wedding, Dr. and Mrs. Howe made an extensive tour of Europe. For five months they lived in Rome, where their first child was born.

On their return to Boston, Dr. Howe bought a large estate near the Institute for the Blind, of which he was a Director, and in this happy home were born five more children. While a devoted mother, Mrs. Howe still found time to continue her studies, reading the Latin poets and the German philosophers, and all the while writing essays and poems for the magazines.

At the age of thirty-five she published her first volume of poems entitled *Passion Flowers*, and two years later, another called *Words for the Hour*. She also assisted her husband in editing the *Boston Commonwealth*, an anti-slavery newspaper, for in this cause both became leaders, being associated with Garrison, Sumner, Phillips, Higginson, and Theodore Parker.

In 1862, Mrs. Howe published in the *Atlantic Monthly* her best known poem, *Battle Hymn of the Republic*. This inspiring hymn reached the prisoners in Libby Prison through Chaplain McCabe, who sang it to celebrate a victory of the Union troops. After Chaplain McCabe was released from prison, and while he was lecturing in Washington, he narrated this incident. This attracted the attention of the public, so that the beautiful hymn soon became

popular throughout the country.   Later, it became
the battle cry of the Union army, being sung by the
men as they marched into action.

When Colonel T. W. Higginson urged Mrs. Howe to
sign a call for a Woman Suffrage Convention to be held
in Boston, she not only signed, but attended the Convention, and later became intimately associated with
the movement, often making speeches on the subject.

She was a delegate to the Congress for Prison
Reform in England, where, besides speaking earnestly
against the flogging of prisoners, she also urged arbi-
tration as the means of settling international disputes.
In her own country, she organized the Women's Peace
Festival, with the object of turning the attention of
women to the horrors and needlessness of war.   Thus
we find this remarkable woman always in the van of
progress and generally much ahead of her time.

In 1876, after a brief illness, Dr. Howe died.   Mrs.
Howe then took her daughter Maud to Europe, where
she remained for two years, trying by travel to dull
the sharp edge of her affliction.   It was at this time
that Mrs. Howe took up the study of Greek, in
which she became very proficient, and the study of
which she kept up until her last illness.

For a long period of years Mrs. Howe lectured and

wrote on subjects which concerned the social improvement of mankind.

Almost her last appearance in public was at the reception given to the representatives of twenty-seven nations by the Hudson-Fulton Celebration Commission at the Metropolitan Opera House, New York City. Mrs. Howe read an original poem written for the occasion. While she read, the entire audience stood respectfully, and as she sat down, all joined in singing the *Battle Hymn of the Republic*. Her really last appearance in public was but two weeks before her death, at the inauguration of the second president of Smith College, at which function she was given the degree of LL. D.

Mrs. Howe died October 18, 1910, at her country place in Portsmouth. She will long be remembered for her work in the anti-slavery cause and for the advancement of woman, for her literary merits, and for her beautiful domestic life.

QUEEN VICTORIA
From an old engraving

QUEEN VICTORIA

(1819 – 1901)

"Her court was pure; her life serene;
God gave her peace; her land reposed;
A thousand claims to reverence closed
In her as Mother, Wife and Queen."

—Alfred Tennyson

On May 24, 1819, a little girl was born in Kensington Palace, London, who received the name of Victoria. Her father, Edward, the Duke of Kent, was the fourth son of King George III.

At the time of Victoria's birth it seemed unlikely that she would ever become queen. Between her and the crown stood three uncles and her father. But when, in January, 1820, within a few days of each other her father and the King died, it began to be seen that Victoria would in all probability become the future ruler of England. In consequence, her education was conducted with the greatest care. Her mother, the Duchess of Kent, devoted herself to the child and made every effort to develop in her all that was good and noble.

Victoria lived a quiet and natural life in the open air, having for instructor a tutor who was a clergyman of the Church of England.   When lessons were over, the little Princess used to go out into Kensington Gardens, where she rode a donkey gaily decked with blue ribbons.   Here she also walked, and would kiss her hand to the children who sometimes gathered about and looked through the railing to see a real Princess.

Victoria was very fond of dolls.   She had one hundred and thirty-two, which she kept in a house of their own.   She herself made their clothes, and the neatness of her needlework surprised all who saw it. The Princess grew up a merry, affectionate, simple-hearted child, thoughtful for the comfort of others, and extremely truthful.

Victoria's baptismal name was Alexandra Victoria. She preferred to be called by the latter name, but to the English people "Victoria" had a foreign sound and was not very popular.   It remained for the Queen to make it illustrious and beloved.

By the death of George IV in 1830, William, Duke of Clarence, came to the throne.   As he had no children who might succeed to the throne, Victoria became the direct heir.   King William was a good-natured, undignified sort of man, often ridiculous in his public actions. He encouraged Victoria to take part in public ceremonies, and if there was a hall to be dedicated, or a bridge to be opened, or a statue unveiled, the little Princess was called upon quite often to act for the King at the ceremony.

William reigned only nine years, expiring one morning in June, 1837, at Saint James's Palace in London.

When a king or queen dies, it is the custom for persons of high rank to go immediately and salute the new king or queen.

As soon as William, therefore, had drawn his last breath, the Archbishop of Canterbury and the Lord Chamberlain went straight to Kensington Palace to notify Victoria that she had succeeded to the throne. It was five o'clock in the morning, and as she had just arisen from bed, she received them in her dressing-robe. Her first words to the Archbishop were, "I beg your Grace to pray for me." There is a pretty picture of this scene in the Tate Gallery in London, representing the two old men on their knees before a young girl of eighteen years, kissing her hands.

And so, at the age of eighteen, Victoria became

Queen of Great Britain and Ireland and the Empire beyond the seas. Though not beautiful, the young Queen was self-possessed, modest and dignified. Every one bore testimony to the dignity and grace of her actions at this time.

Victoria selected as her Prime Minister Lord Melbourne, to whom she was much attached, and who was her trusted adviser for many years. Just eight days after the first anniversary of her accession to the throne, Victoria was crowned in Westminster Abbey, sitting in the chair where so many English monarchs have received their crowns. The coronation was of great splendor. The sun shone brightly as the procession left Buckingham Palace and her Majesty was greeted all along the route with enthusiastic cheers.

When the Queen entered the Abbey, "with eight ladies all in white floating about her like a silvery cloud, she paused as if for breath and clasped her hands." When she knelt to receive the crown, with the sun shining on her fair young head, the beauty and solemnity of the scene impressed every one. The Duchess of Kent, Victoria's mother, was affected to tears. The ceremonies in the Abbey lasted five hours and the Queen looked pale and weary as she drove to the Palace wearing her crown.

Carlyle, who was among the spectators, said: "Poor little Queen! She is at an age when a girl can hardly be trusted to choose a bonnet for herself. Yet a task is laid upon her from which an archangel might shrink."

Many important matters had to be decided by the young Queen, and sometimes serious troubles grew out of her inexperience. However, being sensible and wise beyond her years, her decisions were for the most part just, and with time she became more and more tactful and better able to cope with the difficulties of governing so great a nation.

A matter of great interest to the public was Victoria's marriage. There were many princes willing and anxious to marry the young Queen of England, but Victoria had a mind and will of her own. She remembered with interest her handsome cousin, Prince Albert of Saxe-Coburg-Gotha, who had visited England two years before, while she was still a Princess.

The Duchess of Kent had been fond of this nephew, whose tastes were refined and whose habits were good. Victoria herself remembered him with affection.

Another visit was arranged by King Leopold, and this time Victoria's interest grew into love. One day she summoned the Prince to her room and offered him her hand in marriage. It must have been a trying thing for her to do, but of course a mere Prince could not propose to the Queen of England. Prince Albert was overjoyed, for he loved Victoria.

The Queen announced her engagement to Parliament, and on February 10, 1840, she was married in the Chapel Royal of Saint James's Palace. She wore a white satin gown trimmed with orange blossoms and a veil of Honiton lace costing one thousand pounds, which had been ordered to encourage the lacemakers of Devonshire. Guns were fired, bells rung, and flags waved, when the ceremony was completed.

After the wedding breakfast at Buckingham Palace, Victoria and Albert drove to Windsor Castle, past twenty-two miles of spectators, who shouted and cheered the youthful pair. There was great rejoicing, and dinners were given to thousands of poor people throughout the Kingdom. After three days spent at Windsor, the Queen and the Prince Consort, as Albert was called, returned to London and began their busy life for the state.

Victoria found a wise adviser in her young husband. He was about her own age, and like her, had a sincere desire always to do the right thing. For a while he was not liked in England, owing to his foreign birth, but before long he gained the affections of that exacting people. The married life of Victoria and Albert was one of unusual happiness and beauty, lasting for twenty years, — until 1861. The Prince, in dying, left a family of nine children. The eldest became the Empress of Germany, and the second was the late King Edward.

The death of the Prince Consort made a great change in the life of the Queen. She became very reserved in her widowhood, and her withdrawal from public life lasted a long time, to the displeasure of the English people. She wore mourning for many years, and was averse to presiding over ceremonious Court functions.

Although impetuous and wilful, Victoria was yet quite willing to be advised by older and wiser persons, and the great men of England very soon learned to respect her character and give heed to her wishes. As a Queen, she really reigned; which means that she was the true head and controller of public affairs. Naturally, she could not do it all herself, but she had the fortunate gift of knowing how to choose her helpers. No reign of any English monarch can be reckoned so great as that of Victoria. It was full of great events, which would require several volumes to recite.

In 1849 she paid a visit to Ireland. In 1851 the first great World's Exposition was held in London. In 1853 there was a war with Russia, and in 1857 the Indian Mutiny occurred. Years later, in 1876, Victoria was formally proclaimed Empress of India. This was accomplished by means of the clever management of Lord Beaconsfield, her Prime Minister, who was a Jew named Disraeli, and a very great statesman.

She encouraged artists and literary men. She made Alfred Tennyson the Poet Laureate of England. Some of his most beautiful lines were addressed to her and the Prince Consort.

The Duke of Wellington, victor at Waterloo, where Napoleon was defeated, was her trusted friend and adviser.

England, in Victoria's reign, made great strides in wealth, art, science, and population. Great men clustered around this wonderful little woman and helped make her rule a glorious one. In 1887, when she had been queen for fifty years, England gave herself a great jubilee which was attended by all the great princes and representatives of kings in the world.

Queen Victoria was fond of music, was an excellent

singer, and spoke many languages. When in London she lived at Buckingham Palace, going at times to Windsor Castle, and occasionally to Balmoral Castle in Scotland, where she would throw off the cares of state and live simply as an English gentlewoman. She had another pleasant home on the Isle of Wight, called Osborne House, where she had her last illness.

Victoria died on January 22, 1901, in her eighty-second year. Her reign was the longest in English history, being nearly sixty-four years. It was exceeded in Europe only by Louis XIV of France, who reigned seventy-one years.

The English people mourned Victoria sincerely and deeply. She had added greatly to the extent and glory of her country. She had been a great and wise ruler. She had commanded the respect of every one at home and abroad, and while she did not talk much, her life proved that a woman can rule as well and wisely as a man. Her private life, as mother, wife, and sovereign, has been a noble example.

At her own request, Queen Victoria's funeral was a military one, her body being placed in the mausoleum built for Prince Albert at Frogmore.

FLORENCE NIGHTINGALE

FLORENCE NIGHTINGALE

(1820 – 1910)

"Theirs is a heroism and patriotism no less grand than that
of the bravest soldier they ever nursed back to life and health."
— *Charles R. Skinner*

Florence Nightingale, one of the most illustrious
personages of Queen Victoria's reign, was born in
Florence, Italy, of English parents.   Since they were
visiting that city at the time, they named their little
daughter after the city of her birth.   A sister, also
born in Italy, was named Parthenope after her birth-
place.

The Nightingales were well-to-do people.   They
owned a beautiful country seat in Derbyshire, which
was for many years the residence of Florence and her
parents.   Florence's love for animals and flowers was
second only to her love of humanity.   Very early
she formed the idea of a vocation which should be
lofty and altruistic.

Her acquaintance with Elizabeth Fry did much
to develop this idea.   Mrs. Fry, already famous as

the first woman who made the welfare of women in prison her care, was a preacher of the Quaker sect.

Having decided upon her course, Miss Nightingale began to learn in the hospitals the medical nurse's duties; and, hearing of a German training school for nurses at Kaiserswerth on the Rhine, she went thither and enrolled herself as a "deaconess."

Kaiserswerth had been started in a very small way by Pastor Fleidner. It was a Protestant school, which combined religious teaching with charitable work among the poor and outcast. The Pastor himself was poor, but his devotion to his work attracted many helpers who gave him money to carry it on.

Florence here became interested also· in prison reform, which led her to open a small home for women after they should come out of prison. The few years she spent here brought her face to face with much suffering and want, and taught her how to find and help unfortunate people.

From Kaiserswerth she went to Paris and entered a Catholic Convent to study the methods of the Sisters. While there she learned to respect and admire so greatly the love and devotion of the nuns, that afterwards, in the Crimean War, she called upon them to assist her.   In England once more, Miss Nightingale settled down to a quiet life, devoting herself to the care of the sick and the poor about her.

Living near the Nightingales, were Sidney Herbert and his wife.   Herbert, who afterwards became Lord Herbert of Lea, was made Secretary of War in the English Government.   The post was no sinecure, for almost immediately after his appointment, war broke out between Russia on one side and England, France, and Turkey on the other.

The scene of the fighting was on the border where Turkey and Russia join.   Near this border is the Crimea, a peninsula, whose principal city is Sebastopol.   To capture this city was the object of the fighting in that part of the country, from which fact the whole war is known as the Crimean War.

England had lived in peace since 1815, a period of forty years, and had to some degree lost the practical knowledge of how to conduct a military campaign. The result was a great waste of time, men and stores, through the inexperience of both officers and soldiers. Disaster followed disaster, each treading upon the other's heels.

Finally William Howard Russell, the War Correspondent of the London Times, wrote a strong letter home to England in which he spoke of the suffering of the wounded, saying: "For all I can see, the men die without the least effort to save them."

Food and clothing were lost, or delayed in transport; the surgeons were without lint or bandages or other of the commonest supplies for hospital work. Russell finally asked a question that made a great stir in England:

"Are there no devoted women among us, able and willing to go forth to minister to the sick and suffering soldiers of the East? Are none of the daughters of England at this extreme hour of need ready for such a work of mercy?"

Florence Nightingale heard this clarion cry and immediately wrote to Secretary Herbert offering her services. Her letter crossed one from him offering her the place of Chief Nurse.

It is doubtful if any choice of a person to do a great work has ever been so fortunate and successful as this one. Florence Nightingale, by her studies and her work in Germany and at home, was already well prepared for nursing. Now it was seen that she was an able organizer as well.

All this came as a great surprise to the world, for Miss Nightingale had never been written or talked about very much.   Now, however, every one asked who she was.

She gathered together thirty-eight nurses, ten of whom were Roman Catholic Sisters of Mercy, and they all left England on October 21, 1854.

On landing in France, the fish-women of Boulogne cared for their trunks and luggage with their own hands and saw the Englishwomen safely on the train for Paris, where they made a short stay at the Convent which Florence had visited years before.   Then they set forth for Marseilles, where they took steamer for Scutari, in Turkey.   Every one helped them and no one would take pay for their service.

There was no little fun made in Europe over the nurses, but ridicule changed to admiration when the first news of their work began to reach home.   Miss Nightingale paid no attention either to the shallow fault-finding, or to praise, but went straight ahead to do the work she found in Scutari.   And great need there was of her help!

It might be well here to quote a description of Florence Nightingale:

You cannot hear her say a few sentences, no, not even look at her without feeling that she is an extraordinary being.   Simple, intellectual, sweet, full of love

and benevolence, she is a fascinating and perfect woman. .
She is tall and pale.   Her face is exceedingly lovely, but
better than all is the soul's glory that shines through
every feature.   Nothing can be sweeter than her smile. ·
It is like a sunny day in summer.

It would be difficult and painful to describe the conditions she found existing in the hospital at Scutari. The doctors were so few and so overworked, and the wounded men were so numerous, that many died who might have been saved.   Hospital supplies were there, but could not be found.   Perhaps never in civilized times was there so much unnecessary suffering.

Miss Nightingale and her staff of nurses could do very little compared to the great need, but they took up the work bravely.   Here Miss Nightingale's ability as a manager and director was shown.   She soon came to be ranked with the Generals in ability and power.   All opposition to her as a woman began to fade away as her blessed work among the sick and dying soldiers began to be appreciated.

Soon all England was alive to the great work, and more nurses, and large gifts of supplies and money began to be hurried to the Crimea.

Florence Nightingale spent nearly two years in the Crimea.   Once she fell dangerously ill with a fever.

but the care she had given to others was returned in the form of all manner of attentions to her. She never quite recovered from the effects of that terrible Crimean fever.

When the war was over, she went back to England so quietly that hardly anyone outside her home knew of her return. When it became known, she was overwhelmed by all sorts of people trying to do her honor. Most of them she refused to see. Queen Victoria invited her to come to Balmoral Castle and this honor she could not refuse, for the request of a Queen is a command. The Queen decorated her with a beautiful jewel, treating her simply in the spirit of one woman recognizing another who deserved recognition.

Florence Nightingale lived to be ninety years old, thus spending fifty years in England after the Crimean war.

She devoted all her life to benevolent works: building new hospitals, writing books on the care of the sick, and inspiring many young women to give their lives to the service of humanity. She never married.

At her death it was proposed to bury her in Westminster Abbey, that great final home of England's illustrious sons and daughters, but the honor was declined by her friends, and she sleeps sweetly in the village church-yard near her old country home in Hampshire.

Our own Longfellow wrote these fine lines about Florence Nightingale, referring to her habit of going about the hospitals at night with a lamp in her hand:

> "On England's annals through the long
>   Hereafter of her speech and song,
>   A light its ray shall cast
>   From the portals of the past.
>
> "A lady with a lamp shall stand
>   In the great history of the land;
>   A noble type of good
>   Heroic womanhood."

SUSAN B. ANTHONY

SUSAN B. ANTHONY

(1820 – 1906)

"That one who breaks the way with tears,
Many shall follow with a song."

Among those who believed that in certain lines woman can do as valuable work as man, was Susan B. Anthony. During her long, busy life of eighty-six years, she protested against the injustice done to woman on the part of Society.

It has been truly said that woman's place is in the home, and true it is that most women prefer home life; yet does not every one know that, in numerous instances, women are compelled to earn their own living, and often in addition to support their brothers and sisters, fathers and mothers?

"Why, then," thought Miss Anthony, "should laws be such as to prevent women from having the same opportunities as men in the business world?" This line of thought was early forced upon her.

Born on the fifteenth of February, 1820, in South Adams, Massachusetts, of Quaker ancestry, she re-

ceived a liberal education from her father. Mr.
Anthony being a well-to-do merchant, it was not
supposed that his daughters would ever be obliged
to support themselves, but he believed that girls as
well as boys should be fitted to do so, if the necessity
arose.

The wisdom of Mr. Anthony's course early became
apparent, for when Susan was seventeen years of age,
he failed in business, and his daughters were able
to assist him to retrieve his fortunes.

Susan began to teach in a Quaker family, receiving
the sum of one dollar a week and board.   Later she
taught in the Public Schools of Rochester, to which
place the family had removed.   Here she received
a salary of eight dollars a month for the same work
for which men were paid twenty-five and thirty
dollars.

It was this injustice which first led her to speak
in public.   At a meeting of the New York State
Teachers' Association, she petitioned the Superin-
tendent for equal pay with men, but notwithstanding
the fact that her work was admitted to be entirely
satisfactory, her petition was refused on the ground
that she was a woman.

Miss Anthony worked for years trying to bring the

wages of women workers up to those of men, and although she did not succeed in accomplishing her desire, still by her efforts the general standing of women was greatly improved.

She continued to teach until 1852, but all the while she was taking a keen interest in every reform movement. The more she studied and pondered over the condition of women, the stronger grew her conviction that they would never receive proper pay or recognition, never be able to do the work God intended them to do in the world, unless they should be given equal political rights with man.

Miss Anthony did not at first advocate full suffrage for women; at that period it appeared a thing quite impossible for them to obtain. Wisely she worked for what she believed was within the range of possibility to secure. She was much interested in the temperance movement, and spoke frequently in public for that cause. It happened one day that the Sons of Temperance invited the Daughters of Temperance to their Convention at Albany. The Daughters accepted the invitation and attended, but the Sons would not allow them to speak, — which so angered Miss Anthony and some other women that they left the hall and held a meeting of their own outside. Out of this episode grew the Women's New York State Temperance Society, founded in 1852, and afterward developing into the Women's Christian Temperance Union.

By this time Miss Anthony was well known as a lecturer. But when she actually called a Convention of Women at Albany to urge the public to recognize the wrongs, and demand the rights of her sex, considerable comment followed. In the sixth decade of the Nineteenth Century women had not become so active in public affairs that one of them could call a Convention and the general public take no notice.

The right to vote on educational questions was at length granted women in New York State, and the credit for this is due to Susan B. Anthony and Elizabeth Cady Stanton.

Miss Anthony's friendship with Mrs. Stanton started her in new fields of action. Mrs. Stanton's husband was a lawyer and journalist, who had been a student in Lane Theological Seminary. A noted abolitionist, he went as delegate to the World's Anti-Slavery Convention in London. Mrs. Stanton accompanied him, meeting there Lucretia Mott, who was the sole woman delegate. These two women called the first Woman's Rights Convention at

Seneca Falls in 1848. Though Miss Anthony did not attend this meeting, she later became a complete convert, being already headed in the direction of woman's political and social emancipation.

As soon as Miss Anthony became convinced that only through the use of the ballot could woman succeed in obtaining the same rights in the business world as men, she entered heart and soul into the work of securing it, going to many cities of the North and the South to lecture, often speaking five or six times a week. Her platform manner was direct, straight-forward, and convincing; her good humor, unfailing; her quickness to see and grasp an opportunity for retort, noteworthy.

In 1860 the New York Legislature passed a bill giving to married women the possession of their earnings and the guardianship of their children. This was largely due to Miss Anthony's exertions. For many years she had kept up a constant agitation on the injustice of depriving women of these fundamental rights.

Belonging to the Abolition Party, she had worked during the war with the Women's Loyal Legion for the abolition of slavery. In 1867 Mrs. Stanton, Lucy Stone and Susan B. Anthony went to Kansas

in the interests of woman suffrage; there the three
women secured nine thousand votes in favor of the
cause.   Their work, however, had no immediately vis-
ible effect, but to-day, forty-five years later, women
in that State enjoy the privilege of the ballot.

As a citizen of Rochester wishing to test her right
to the suffrage, she voted at the National election of
1872.   For so doing she was arrested, tried, and
fined one hundred dollars and costs.   With her
characteristic defiance of injustice, Miss Anthony
refused to pay the fine, which to this day remains
unpaid.

Beloved by her co-workers, to strangers Miss
Anthony appeared stern and uncompromising.   Yet
all her friends testify to her lovable qualities and
generous nature.   Mrs. Stanton, her intimate friend
for eighteen years, said of her:

> She is earnest, unselfish, and as true to principle as
> the needle to the pole.   I have never known her to do
> or say a mean or narrow thing; she is entirely above
> that petty envy and jealousy that mar the character of
> so many otherwise good women.

Miss Anthony herself said, "My work is like subsoil
ploughing — preparing the way for others to perfect."

But the last eight years of her long life, in which

she worked constantly and achieved much, must have given her the satisfaction of knowing that all the "subsoil ploughing" had not been in vain. Her constancy in keeping the idea of votes for women before the public won many over to the cause, and paved the way for the partial victory of to-day. At present, women have the privilege of the ballot in ten States of the Union: California, Colorado, Idaho, Utah, Wyoming, Washington, Arizona, Oregon, Kansas, and Michigan. It is clear that the question of woman suffrage has ceased to be a mere matter of academic discussion and that it is a very practical and even vital issue to-day.

For years Miss Anthony endured cruel misrepresentation and ridicule; now she is acknowledged to have been a woman of splendid intellect and wonderful courage, who devoted her life to the betterment of humanity.

To her co-workers she was always "Aunt Susan," and when her last illness came, there were many loving friends to care for her. The Reverend Anna Howard Shaw was with her when she died at Rochester, March 16, 1906. She says, "Miss Anthony died with calmness and courage. She spent her life in making other women freer and happier."

MARY A. LIVERMORE

MARY A. LIVERMORE

(1821–1905)

"I am not accustomed to the language of eulogy. I have
never studied the art of paying compliments to women. But I
must say that if all that has been said by orators and poets
since the Creation of the World, in praise of women, was
applied to the women of America, it would not do them justice
for their conduct during this war. I will close by saying, God
bless the women of America."

— Abraham Lincoln

The life of Mary A. Livermore shows how a poor,
unknown girl became famous, the world over, as
an orator and reformer.

Mary Rice was born in Boston, Massachusetts, December 19, 1821. Her parents were stern Calvinists,
her grandfathers for six generations having been Welsh
preachers. Hence, Mary was brought up "after the
strictest sect a Pharisee." She was a restless, active
child, fond of play, yet interested in work. At an early
age she was sent to a Public School in Boston, where
she made rapid progress in her studies, being quick to
learn and persistent and enthusiastic over her tasks.

Her class-mates were fond of her, and by reason of an unusually strong character, she became a leader among them.   The poor or unfortunate always appealed to her.   If ever a girl appeared in the school wearing shabby clothes or eating a scanty luncheon, Mary would manage to prevent her from feeling uncomfortable.   It is not surprising that she was a favorite.

In out-of-door sports she excelled most of the girls, being famous for running, jumping and sliding.   One day, after she had spent a happy hour at her favorite sport of sliding on the ice, she ran into the house exclaiming, "Splendid, splendid sliding!"

Her father replied, "Yes, Mary, it is good fun, but hard on the shoes!"

This led the child to believe that her father's burden was increased by her amusement, so she decided that she would never slide again.   When ten years of age she grew so deeply anxious for the spiritual welfare of her five little brothers and sisters that she could not sleep.   She would crawl out of bed at night and beg her father and mother to arise and pray for their conversion, once saying: "It is no matter about me; if they can be saved, I can bear anything."

Even in her play she would devise means of instructing as well as entertaining the children. There being no money to buy toys for them, Mary introduced the game of playing school. It is said that she imitated her own teacher to perfection. Sometimes in the old woodshed she arranged the logs to represent the pews of a church, and desiring a larger audience than that of the children, she stood up sticks of wood to represent people. Then, when the assemblage was sufficiently large to warrant a service, she would conduct one herself, praying and preaching with the utmost seriousness.

Her mother, surprised at her ability in this line, once said to her, "Mary, I wish you had been a boy; you could have been trained for the ministry!"

In those days no one even thought of educating a girl to speak from the pulpit, though to-day it is not uncommon; nor could Mrs. Rice dream that her daughter would one day become a powerful public speaker in an important cause, and deliver speeches in lecture halls and churches.

When Mary was twelve, she resolved to assist her father in supporting the large family, for she had observed with sorrow how hard he worked. Dressmaking seemed to offer good opportunities, so she entered a shop as apprentice. In three months she had learned her trade, and was then hired at thirty-seven cents a day to work three months more, but being desirous of earning more money, she engaged to make a dozen flannel shirts at home for a clothier. After sewing all day in the shop and sitting up at home until early morning hours, she could not finish the shirts in the time agreed upon.

One evening the man called for them, greatly to Mrs. Rice's surprise, for she had known nothing about Mary's plan. Mary explained the delay, promising to have the shirts finished the next day. When the clothier had left, Mrs. Rice burst into tears. "We are not so poor as that, my dear child! What will become of you if you take all the cares of the world upon you?" she said.

Mary completed the shirts, took them to the clothier and received the sum of seventy-five cents. This ended her experience as a seamstress, for her mother would not permit the child to continue such work.

At fourteen, Mary was graduated from the Public School, receiving a gold medal for good scholarship. She then entered the Charlestown Female Seminary, where she became one of the best scholars in the institution. Her ability was so pronounced, that when one of the teachers died, she was at once asked to take the vacant position. She conducted her class with much tact and wisdom, earning enough to pay for the four year course, which she completed in two, by studying and reciting out of school hours.

At the age of eighteen, she took a position as governess in the family of a wealthy Virginia planter. Her object was not altogether teaching; she wished to investigate for herself the slavery question, which was then much discussed by Abolitionists. She had heard the lectures of Lucretia Mott and John G. Whittier and determined to find out if the facts were as bad as stated. Her two years' experience in Virginia made her an uncompromising Abolitionist.

The faculty of the Duxbury High School was in need of a Principal. It was customary to place men in such positions, but Mary Rice's fame had made its way to Duxbury. They had heard of her as an unusual young woman and one of the most learned of the day. So Mary was placed over the High School, and there she remained until she was twenty-three years old, when she resigned to become the wife of the Reverend D. P. Livermore, a young minister, two years her senior, whose church was near her school.

Mary immediately began to coöperate with Dr.

Livermore in his work. For thirteen years she assisted him in the affairs of his parish, during which time three children were born to them. She started literary and benevolent societies among the church members and was active in the cause of temperance, organizing a club of fifteen hundred boys and girls which she called the "Cold Water Army."

In 1857 the Livermores removed to Chicago. Mrs. Livermore while there aided in editing the *New Covenant*, a religious paper, at the same time writing stories and sketches for many Eastern publications. In 1860, when Abraham Lincoln was nominated for the Presidency, Mrs. Livermore was the only woman present,— probably the first woman representative of the press who ever reported a political convention.

The breaking out of the Civil War changed her life of domestic quietness to public activity. Being in Boston at the time that the President called for volunteer troops, she witnessed their departure for the seat of war. The sad scenes at the station, where mothers parted from sons, and wives from their husbands, affected her strongly. As the train carrying the soldiers started off, some of the women fainted. Mrs. Livermore helped to revive them, telling them not to grieve, but rather to be thankful that they had sons to fight for their country. For her part, she told them, she grieved to have no son to send.

Then a question arose in her mind: What *could* women do to help? The general feeling seemed to be that women could do nothing, since they were not allowed to enlist and fight as soldiers. They were told they were not wanted in the hospitals, but not-¦ withstanding this a large number of women banded together and formed "The United States Sanitary Commission," whose object was to provide bedding, clothing, food, and comforts for the soldiers in camp, and supplies for the wounded in the hospitals.

Branch associations were formed in ten large cities. Mrs. Livermore and Mrs. Jane C. Hoge were put in charge of the Northwestern branch. Together with others Mrs. Livermore went to Washington to talk with President Lincoln. They asked him the question, "May women go to the front?"

Lincoln replied, "The *law* does not *grant* to any civilian, either man or woman, the privilege of going to the front."

The emphasis he placed upon the words *law* and *grant* convinced these women that he would not disapprove of their plans. So Mrs. Livermore entered hand, heart and soul into the work of relief.

The North was entirely unprepared for war. , The hospitals were few and poorly equipped; nurses were scarce and not well trained; there were no diet kitchens; nor was there any way of supplying proper medicines to the sick or of caring for the wounded. To all of these matters Mrs. Livermore gave her attention; the confusion came to an end, and soon the machinery of the new department was running smoothly.

She formed soldiers' aid societies; enlisted nurses for the hospitals and took them to their posts; she went to the front with supplies, and saw that they were properly distributed; she nursed and cheered the wounded soldiers, and often brought back invalids with her to their homes. With all this work, she kept cheerful and well, and found time to write letters of comfort and cheer to the families of the sick. In one year she wrote seventeen hundred letters, many being from dying soldiers, and containing their last farewell to loved ones at home.

The Sanitary Commission was permitted in time of battle to keep its wagons in the rear of the army. Hot soup and hot coffee were kept in readiness, cool water and medicines were given when necessary, while the mere fact that brave women were ready to assist the wounded, put confidence into the hearts of the men.

It is impossible to describe the great work done by this untiring woman. Mrs. Livermore tells about it in her book called *My Story of the War*, which is said to be the best account of the hospital and sanitary work of the Civil War that has ever been written.

This work took a great deal of money. Donations must be constantly solicited and Sanitary Fairs arranged. From all parts of the country, people were writing and begging Mrs. Livermore to come to them and tell them about her plans. She frequently did describe them in an informal way to small audiences.

Her first public speech was made in Dubuque, Iowa, where she had consented to address some ladies. Leaving Chicago by the night train she reached the Mississippi River at a point where there was no bridge, travelers being obliged to cross by ferry. It was very cold and the ice in the river had stopped the ferryboats. Mrs. Livermore, after waiting nearly all day, began to think she would not be able to keep her engagement. At last she saw two men starting out in a small boat, whom she asked to row her across.

One man said, "No, we can't think of it! You'll be drowned!"

Mrs. Livermore replied, "I can't see that I shall be drowned any more than you!"

Her offer to pay them well settled the matter. This determination to accomplish whatever she undertook to do was the chief reason for Mrs. Livermore's success in all her undertakings. The fact is, she liked to do hard things.

Upon her arrival at Dubuque she found that the ladies had made great preparations to receive her. They had invited the Governor of the State and many noted men, and the largest church in town was crowded with eager people. This rather alarmed her. At first she refused to speak, saying that she had come to talk to a few ladies only; that she had never made a speech in her life. But when they said that by speaking she might be the means of inducing the great State of Iowa to enter upon the work of Sanitary Relief, her shyness departed and she held her audience spellbound for an hour and a quarter. A new power had suddenly developed in her.

At the close of her address the Governor of the State arose and said,

"Mrs. Livermore has told us of the soldiers' needs

and of our duties! It is now our turn to speak, and we must speak in dollars and gifts!"

The enthusiasm was great; eight thousand dollars was soon pledged and other donations were made. It was decided to hold a Sanitary Fair in Dubuque, and Mrs. Livermore was engaged to speak in different towns throughout the State to interest the people in it. When the fair was held, sixty thousand dollars was cleared. After that, Mary Livermore was never again afraid to speak before a large audience. By her lectures she raised hundreds of thousands of dollars for the hospital work.

At the close of the war, people were so anxious to hear Mrs. Livermore that she became a regular public lecturer, traveling from place to place and lecturing always before crowded houses. Her eloquence has been equaled by few modern speakers, and undoubtedly she was the foremost of women orators.

Before the war, Mrs. Livermore had been opposed to woman suffrage, but life in the army caused her to change her views on that question. She saw that, under existing political and social conditions, women could never hope to complete reforms until they possessed the right to vote. She was also devoted to the cause of temperance, serving for ten years as President of the Women's Christian Temperance Union of Massachusetts. All this while she was writing articles for magazines, and at the age of seventy-five Mrs. Livermore produced a book of seven hundred pages, entitled *The Story of My Life*.

A bust of Mrs. Livermore, made by the sculptor, Annie Whitney, was presented to the Shurtleff School in Boston by the Alumnae Association of that institution. It stands opposite that of Lucy Stone, which was the first bust of a woman ever accepted by the city of Boston for its schools.

Mrs. Livermore continued in public work, while living at her beautiful home in Melrose, Massachusetts, until May 23, 1905, when she passed away at the age of eighty-four.

CLARA BARTON

CLARA BARTON

(1821 – 1912)

"She was on the firing line for humanity all her life."

The Red Cross Society, whose object is to relieve the sufferings caused by war, is well known the world over, and the name of Clara Barton must ever be associated with it.

This Society was founded in Europe in 1864, but did not make its way to America until 1881, when Clara Barton succeeded in establishing it.

Born in the town of North Oxford, Massachusetts, on Christmas Day, 1821, Clara Barton began life under most favorable circumstances.

The family was well-to-do and Clara, being the youngest, received much attention from all. Her father, who had fought under Mad Anthony Wayne against the Indians of the West, used to tell her stories of army life — knowledge which she afterward turned to good account.

Her elder brother was fond of mathematics, and insisted upon teaching Clara the mysteries of number. These she mastered rapidly and soon no toy equaled her little slate in her esteem.

Her younger brother, David, was a fearless and daring rider. On the farm were several fine horses, for Mr. Barton was fond of the animals and raised his own colts. It was David's delight to take little Clara, throw her upon the back of a colt and spring upon another himself. Then, shouting to her to "cling fast to the mane," he would catch hold of her by one foot and together they would gallop away. What mad rides they took, and how well Clara learned to stick on a horse's back! These lessons, too, she had cause to be thankful for later in life, when she was obliged to mount a strange horse on the battle-field and ride fearlessly to a place of safety.

Her two sisters, who were teachers, took care that she should have a knowledge of books. Miss Barton said that she did not remember the time when she could not read; she always did her own story reading.

When old enough she was sent to an academy at Clinton, New York, where she graduated. She then became a teacher and opened the first free school in the State of New Jersey, at Bordentown. Here her work was very successful, her school numbering at the close of the first year six hundred pupils. But, her health failing, she gave up the school work in 1854 and obtained a position as Head Clerk in the Patent Office at Washington.

When the Civil War broke out, she offered her services as a volunteer nurse, and from the beginning of the war until its close she worked in the hospital, in the camp, and on the battle-field.

During the Peninsula campaign in 1862, Miss Barton faced horrible scenes on the field. She also served eight months in the hospitals on Morris Island during the siege of Charleston, and was at the front during the Wilderness campaign. In 1864 she was put in charge of the hospitals at the front of the Army of the James, and continued that work until the close of the war.

All this time Miss Barton persisted in aiding the wounded soldiers of *both* armies — a practice which shocked many people and caused them to protest. But she paid no attention to the protests, nor are any such heard to-day, for Clara Barton's way of helping the suffering, regardless of the uniform they wore, is now followed over the civilized world; it is the very heart of the plan of the Red Cross Society itself.

War over, and peace assured to our land, President Lincoln requested Miss Barton to search for the eighty thousand men whose names were on the army records, but of whom no trace could be found. In the course of this work, Miss Barton visited the prison at Andersonville and helped the released prisoners to regain their health and their homes. She laid out the ground of the National Cemetery at that place, identified the dead, and caused marked gravestones to be placed over the bodies of twelve thousand nine hundred men. Four hundred tablets, marked "Unknown," were placed over the bodies of other dead soldiers.

This work took four years to accomplish, and when it was over Miss Barton went to Switzerland for rest. Here she first heard of the Red Cross Society. The idea had originated with a Swiss, M. Henri Dunant. Each European country had signed a treaty permitting the members of this association to help all the wounded on the battle-field without interference, and without regard to religion or race, or whether they were friends or foes.

Miss Barton devoted herself to this work during the Franco-Prussian War. After the siege of Strasburg, when the people of that city were in a terrible condition, she organized a relief fund for the starving, and saw to it that the homeless were given places to sleep. Materials for garments were obtained, and the poor women were set to work at a fair price to make articles of wearing apparel for the needy.

When no longer needed in Strasburg, Miss Barton went to Paris, where the breaking out of the French Revolution after the war with Prussia had caused great distress. She entered the city on foot, for it was impossible to procure a horse, thousands having been slain to use as food for the starving inhabitants. Miss Barton immediately began relief work there, with such success that she came to be looked upon as an angel.

In 1873, on her return to America, she asked Congress to join in a treaty with the European powers to establish the Red Cross Society here. It took a long time to secure this legislation, and it was not until 1881, as stated before, that the Red Cross was established with us. Clara Barton was chosen as the first President and soon afterward she had an amendment passed widening the scope of the Society so as to include cases of suffering from floods, fires, famine, earthquake, and other forms of disaster. The amendment also gave protection to all Red Cross workers. This was agreed to at a conference of the Society held at Berne in 1882, but was not adopted by any of the European nations.   At that time there was little possibility of a war in the United States, and Miss Barton thought she would have little to do unless she extended the plan of work.   As it was, she found quite enough to do.

The forest fires in Michigan, the Mississippi Valley floods, 1882–1883, the Charleston earthquake, the Johnstown flood — all afforded much work for the Red Cross.   During the famine in Russia, 1891-1892, Miss Barton and her Society took an active part in distributing food and clothing.   When the frightful massacres in Armenia brought horror to the civilized world, again Miss Barton made an appeal to a European country to be allowed to help the sufferers. The Sultan at first objected, but public opinion was too strong for him, and he finally consented on condition that the workers should place the crescent above the cross on the badges worn by them.   Miss Barton and her assistants were then pleasantly received and succeeded in giving valuable aid.

In 1898 President McKinley sent Miss Barton to Cuba to help the poor people of that country, many of whom were starving.   During the Cuban War which followed, she went to the battle-fields and did heroic work there.

When the Galveston flood occurred, Miss Barton was eighty years old. Yet to Galveston she hastened. The strain, however, was more than she could endure. From that time she gave up active work and made her home in Glen Echo, a small village in Maryland. Here, enjoying the companionship of a few faithful friends, she spent the remainder of her life, passing away on April 12, 1912.

Miss Barton possessed one of the most remarkable collections of medals and other decorations in existence. They were presented to her by nearly every country on the globe. Many are set with rare jewels and bear inscriptions. Among them is the Iron Cross of Germany, the highest honor Germany can bestow, and one conferred only for deeds of great personal bravery. A rare jewel, which Miss Barton always wore, was a pansy cut from a single amethyst, presented to her by the Grand Duchess of Baden in memory of their lifelong friendship.

Clara Barton ranks as one of the greatest heroines the world has known. Her name is known and loved throughout Europe and America for unselfish devotion to a great cause. Her services in foreign lands were offered as freely as in her own country, for her creed was the brotherhood of man.

HARRIET HOSMER

HARRIET HOSMER

(1830 – 1908)

. . . "A sculptor wields
The chisel, and the stricken marble grows
To beauty." . . .

— *Bryan*

Harriet Goodhue Hosmer was born in Watertown, Massachusetts, October 9, 1830.   She was the youngest child of Hiram and Sarah Grant Hosmer.   From her father came her marked independence of character; from her mother, her imagination and artistic tastes.

The latter died when Harriet was four years of age. Dr. Hosmer determined to save his daughters from the insidious disease which had carried away his two sons as well as his wife, and so instituted for them a system of physical training, insisting upon out-of-door sports and amusements.   Notwithstanding all his efforts, however, the elder daughter died, leaving Harriet as the sole surviving child.

Dr. Hosmer, grieved, but undismayed, renewed his

endeavors to strengthen Harriet's vigor and increase her powers of endurance.   Harriet took to this treatment very kindly, spending many joyous days tramping through the woods with her dogs.   All the while, she observed keenly, acquiring a knowledge of plant and animal life, and storing up impressions of the beautiful and harmonious in Nature.

Her home was situated on the Charles River.   She had her own boathouse and bathhouse.   In summer she rowed and swam; in winter she skated.   No nook or corner of the country round was unknown to her; the steepest hills, the wildest and most rugged regions, were her familiar haunts.   A madcap was Harriet, and the sober neighbors were often astonished and even scandalized, by the undignified speed she made on her beautiful horse.

This kind of life would always have satisfied her, and Harriet thought it nothing short of an affliction when her father said she must go to school.   Was she not getting her education in riding about the country?   However, to school she went, in Boston, for several years.

But when she reached the age of fifteen, Dr. Hosmer became convinced that Harriet would never thrive, mentally or physically, unless she were left free to follow her own bent.   And perhaps he never in his life made a wiser decision.

So he sent the wild girl to the home school of Mrs. Charles Sedgwick of Lenox.   Here she had the benefits of cultured and elevating surroundings, together with motherly care, and also of the out-of-door life so dear to her heart and so necessary to her well-being.

Lenox, in the beautiful Berkshire Hills, was at that time a primitive village, though it has since grown into a fashionable summer resort.   There, in Mrs. Sedgwick's refined and peaceful home, Harriet acquired her real education from listening to the conversations of such men and women as Nathaniel Hawthorne, Ralph Waldo Emerson, Frederika Bremer and Fanny Kemble.

This stimulus was all Harriet needed to develop in her the idea of doing some serious work in life. She began to give a great deal of time to drawing, her study of nature and her splendid powers of observation being of great assistance to her here.

Those were happy days for Harriet.   She was the life of the household, being always ready to deliver comic lectures, to dress up in odd costumes, to give impromptu theatricals, or to say or do original things.   Mrs. Kemble, who occupied a villa near the Sedgwicks, often entertained the schoolgirls by reading and reciting Shakespeare to them. Harriet became devotedly attached to her, their friendship lasting throughout their lives.

In 1849, Harriet left Lenox and returned to Watertown for the purpose of beginning her life-work, which she had decided should be that of a sculptor. To work intelligently, it was necessary for her to know anatomy thoroughly, but there was no college where she could prepare herself in that study, for the subject was at that time reserved strictly for men.

It happened that Harriet went to St. Louis to visit friends, and that while she was there some lectures on anatomy were delivered by Dr. J. N. McDowell, the head of the medical department of the State University. The lectures were not open to women, but so great was Harriet's desire to profit by them that Professor McDowell allowed her to see his notes and examine the specimens by herself — a very radical act on his part, since it was thought indelicate for a woman to study this noble subject, even though the knowledge was to be used to create the beautiful in art and, so, to elevate public thought.

Harriet studied hard, and was rewarded at the close of the term by receiving her diploma with the class. This great concession had been gained through the influence of Mr. Wayman Crow, the father of a classmate of Harriet. Mr. Crow became her intimate friend and close adviser, watching over her and guiding her affairs as long as he lived.

The coveted diploma secured, Miss Hosmer decided to travel before returning home. She visited New Orleans and traversed almost the entire length of the Mississippi River. While on a Mississippi steamboat, some young men began to talk of their chances for reaching the top of a certain bluff which they were then approaching. Miss Hosmer made a wager that she could reach it before any of them. The race was made, Miss Hosmer winning easily. The bluff, about five hundred feet in height, was straightway named Mount Hosmer.

In 1852 appeared her first finished product. This was the bust of a beautiful maiden just falling asleep, and was entitled *Hesper, the Evening Star.*

About this time Miss Hosmer met the renowned actress, Charlotte Cushman. Miss Cushman, seeing promise in the girl's work, urged her to go to Rome and study. Dr. Hosmer approved of this suggestion, and soon father and daughter sailed for Europe.

Upon their arrival in Rome, they called upon John Gibson, the most noted English sculptor of the day, to whom they had letters of introduction.   After examining the photographs of *Hesper*, and talking with Harriet, who always impressed strangers with a sense of her ability and earnestness, Gibson consented to take her into his studio as a pupil.

Overjoyed was she to be assigned to a small room formerly occupied by Canova, of whom Gibson had been a pupil.   Here she began the study of ancient classical art, making copies of many masterpieces and selling them without any trouble.   When her first large order for a statue came from her friend, Mr. Wayman Crow, Harriet felt that she was beginning the world in earnest.   When this order was soon afterward followed by another for a statue to be placed in the Library at St. Louis, she knew that her career as a sculptor was assured.

International fame came to her with a figure of *Puck*, copies of which found their way into important public galleries and into private collections on both continents.

When the State of Missouri decided to erect its first public monument, she was requested to design a statue of Thomas H. Benton, to be cast in bronze and placed in St. Louis.

A work attracting unusual attention was *Zenobia*,

Queen of Palmyra, in Chains. A replica of this now stands in the Metropolitan Museum, of New York City. Miss Hosmer's whole soul was enlisted in her work on this particular piece of sculpture. She spent days searching the libraries for information upon the subject, information that should stimulate her hand to express powerfully ‑her conception of the great queen — dignified, imposing, and courageous, despite her fallen fortunes. This statue was exhibited in Rome, England and America.

Harriet Hosmer possessed a great faculty for inspiring warm and lasting friendships. Among her intimate friends during her long residence in Italy were the Brownings, Mrs. Jameson, Sir Frederick Leighton, and W. W. Story. The charming group of artistic people living at that time in Rome, most of them engaged in earnest work, occasionally took a holiday in the form of a picnic or an excursion to the Campagna. In one of her letters Mrs. Browning speaks of these excursions, which had been instituted by Fanny Kemble and her sister, Adelaide Sartoris:

Certainly they gave us some exquisite hours on the Campagna with certain of their friends. Their talk was almost too brilliant. I should mention, too, Miss Hosmer (but she is better than a talker), the young American sculptress who is a great pet of mine and Robert's. She lives here all alone (at twenty-two), works from six o'clock in the morning till night as a great artist must, and this with an absence of pretension and simplicity of manners, which accord rather with the childish dimples in her rosy cheeks, than with her broad forehead and lofty aims.

Frances Power Cobbe wrote of her:

She was in those days the most bewitching sprite the world ever saw. Never have I laughed so helplessly as at the infinite fun of that bright Yankee girl. Even in later years when we perforce grew a little graver, she needed only to begin one of her descriptive stories to make us all young again.

During five happy years, Charlotte Cushman, Miss Hosmer and another friend made their home together. In a letter to America, Harriet wrote: "Miss Cushman is like a mother to me, and spoils me utterly."

In 1862, Miss Hosmer received the news of her father's death. Though grieving sincerely, she worked but the more assiduously, to keep herself free of selfish sorrow. By means of the moderate fortune left her, she was able to take an apartment of her own, and establish a studio which was considered the most beautiful in Rome.

Here she entertained noted people of the day, who came to visit her. Usually, after a hard day's work, she would mount her horse and gallop over the Campagna, returning refreshed at night and ready to dine with her friends. Her animation and wit in discussion, her musical laughter, her gaiety and lightness of spirits, astonished and charmed all who met her.

Like most thinking women of the time, Harriet Hosmer abhorred slavery, and did her part in the Abolition movement by making an inspiring statue called *The African Sibyl* — the figure of a negro girl prophesying the freedom of her race. Of this work, Tennyson said, "It is the most poetic rendering in art of a great historical truth I have ever seen."

One of her notable orders came from the beautiful Queen of Naples, whose portrait she executed in marble. The Queen became a close friend of Miss Hosmer, and her brother, King Ludwig II of Bavaria, frequently visited the studio.

Miss Hosmer's last years were spent in England and America, with only occasional visits to Rome. Death came to her in 1908, at the age of seventy-eight, but to the end she remained an entertaining talker, recalling with joy the many episodes of her busy, happy life and the great people she had known.

LOUISA MAY ALCOTT

LOUISA MAY ALCOTT

(1832–1888)

"God bless all good women! To their soft hands and pity-
ing hearts we must all come at last."

— *Oliver Wendell Holmes*

The following is said to be a description of Louisa
May Alcott at the age of fifteen, written by herself and published in her book called *Little Women.*
She is supposed to be *Jo,* and her three sisters were
the other *little women.*

Jo was very tall, thin and brown, and reminded one
of a colt, for she never seemed to know what to do with
her long limbs, which were very much in the way. She
had a decided mouth, a comical nose, and sharp grey
eyes which appeared to see everything, and were by turns
fierce or funny or thoughtful. Her long, thick hair was
her one beauty, but it was usually bundled into a net
to be out of her way. Round shoulders had Jo, and big
hands and feet, a fly-away look to her clothes, and the
uncomfortable appearance of a girl who was rapidly
shooting up into a woman and didn't like it.

Louisa May Alcott was born November 29th, 1832,

in Germantown, Pennsylvania. Her father was Amos Bronson Alcott, a remarkable man, known as a philosopher and educator. His views of education differed from those of most people of his time, though many of his ideas are highly thought of to-day.

He became an important member of that circle of great men of Concord known as Transcendentalists, and he counted Ralph Waldo Emerson and Henry D. Thoreau among his closest friends.

Miss Alcott's mother was the daughter of Col. Joseph May of Boston and the sister of the Rev. Samuel J. May, a noted anti-slavery leader. Mrs. Alcott was a quiet, unassuming woman, intellectual in her tastes, and accustomed from her childhood to the companionship of cultured people. Although an excellent writer, both in prose and verse, her home and her children were always her first thought. She herself never became publicly known, but her influence may be traced in the lives and works of her brilliant daughter and gifted husband. It is doubtful whether either could have achieved success without her guidance and sympathy.

Thus Louisa came into the world blessed with a heritage of culture and intellect. Her disposition was sunny and cheerful. Upon one occasion, when scarcely able to speak so as to be understood, she suddenly exclaimed at the breakfast table, "I lub everybody in dis whole world!" — an utterance that gives the keynote to her character and nature.

When she was about two years of age, her parents removed to Boston, where Mr. Alcott opened a school. The journey was made by sea. Louisa liked steam-travel so well that she undertook to investigate it thoroughly. To the alarm of her parents, she disappeared, being found after a search in the engine room, sublimely unconscious of soiled clothes, and deeply interested in the machinery.

Her father believed in play as an important means of education, so Louisa and her sister were encouraged in their games. Her doll was to her a real, live baby, to be dressed and undressed regularly, punished when naughty, praised and rewarded when good. She made hats and gowns for it, pretended it was ill, put it to bed, and sent for the doctor, just as any other normal little girl does.

The family cat also came in for its share of attention at the hands of Louisa. No one was allowed to abuse or torment pussy, but the children might "play baby" with her, and rock her to sleep; or they might play that she was sick and that she died, and then attend her funeral.

All this sort of thing Mr. Alcott called "imitation," and at a time when many good parents looked disapprovingly on children's sports, Mr. Alcott placed them in his system of education. These plays were so real to Louisa that she never forgot her joy in them, and years afterward she gave them out delightfully to other children in her stories.

At seven years of age she began, under her father's direction, a daily journal. She would write down the little happenings of her life, her opinions on current events, on books she read, and the conversations she heard. This was good training for the future writer, developing the power of accurate thought and of clear and charming expression.

In 1840, it became evident to Mr. Alcott that he could not remain in Boston. His views on religion and education were so much in advance of the people about him that his school suffered. Concord had long attracted the Alcott family, not only because it was the home of Emerson and others of high intellectual attainments, but because it offered a simple life and rural surroundings. And so it came that the family removed there, occupying a small house known as the Hosmer Cottage, about a mile from Mr. Emerson's home.

At that time there were three Alcott children: Anna, nine years of age, Louisa, eight, and Elizabeth, five years. A boy, born in Boston, died early. A fourth girl, named Abby May, was born in Hosmer Cottage. These four sisters lived a happy life at Concord, although the family had a hard struggle with poverty; for Mr. Alcott, always a poor business man, had lost the little he had in trying to form a model colony, called Fruitlands.

But all were devoted to one another. The children made merry over misfortune, and wooed good luck by refusing to be discouraged. They were always ready to help others, notwithstanding their own poverty. Once, at their mother's suggestion, they carried their breakfast to a starving family, and at another time they contributed their entire dinner to a neighbor who had been caught unprepared when distinguished guests arrived unexpectedly.

Mr. Alcott first attempted to earn his living by working in the fields for his neighbors, and by cultivating his own acre of ground; but this work being uncongenial, he soon drifted into his true sphere — that of writing and lecturing. He supervised the

instruction of all his children, but becoming convinced of Louisa's exceptional ability, he took sole
charge of her education, and except for two brief
periods she was never permitted to attend school.

He was a peculiar man, this Mr. Alcott. One of
his methods of guiding his children was to write
letters to them instead of talking. The talks they
might forget, he said, but the letters they could
keep and read over frequently. Louisa had one
letter from him on *Conscience*, which helped to
mold her whole life.

Mrs. Alcott, too, would sometimes write to Louisa,
giving her some advice or calling her attention to a
fault or undesirable habit. On Louisa's tenth birthday her mother wrote her as follows:

DEAR DAUGHTER:
  Your tenth birthday has arrived. May it be a happy
one, and on each returning birthday may you feel new
strength and resolution to be gentle with sisters, obedient
to parents, loving to every one, and happy in yourself.
  I give you the pencil case I promised, for I have observed that you are fond of writing, and wish to encourage
the habit. Go on trying, dear, and each day it will be
easier to be and do good. You must help yourself, for the
cause of your little troubles is in yourself; and patience
and courage only will make you what mother prays to
see you, a good and happy girl.

To another letter, received on her eleventh birth-day, Louisa replied by writing these verses:

> I hope that soon, dear mother,
>   You and I may be
> In the quiet room my fancy
>   Has so often made for thee —
>
> The pleasant sunny chamber,
>   The cushioned easy-chair,
> The book laid for your reading,
>   The vase of flowers fair;
>
> The desk beside the window
>   When the sun shines warm and bright,
> And there in ease and quiet
>   The promised book you write
>
> While I sit close behind you,
>   Content at last to see
> That you can rest, dear mother,
>   And I can cherish thee.

Louisa very early took upon herself the task of building up the family fortunes. When only fifteen, she began teaching school in a barn. Among her pupils were the children of Mr. Emerson. At this same period we find her writing fairy stories which she sent out to various editors. The editors promptly published these stories, but they sent her no money for

them. But money she must have, so, besides her
teaching, this enterprising girl took in sewing, which
brought her little, but was better than writing stories
for nothing! Louisa's intellect and ability did not
make her vain; she was not ashamed to do any kind
of honorable work.

Since the father proved a failure in supporting the
family, Mrs. Alcott tried to earn something by keeping an intelligence office as an agent for the Over-
seers of the Poor. One day a gentleman called who
wanted "an agreeable companion" for his father and
sister. The companion would be expected to do light
housework, he said, but she would be kindly treated.

Mrs. Alcott could think of no one to fill the position. Then Louisa said, "Mother, why couldn't I
go?"

She did go, remained two months, and was treated
very unkindly, being obliged to do the drudgery of
the entire household. After returning home, she
wrote a story that had a large sale, entitled *How I
Went out to Service.* Surely Louisa Alcott had the
ability to make the best of things, and to turn trials
into blessings.

At nineteen she developed great interest in the
theatre and straightway decided to become an ac-

tress. During her childhood she had written plays which her sister Anna and a few other children acted, to the amusement of the elder members of the family. Now she dramatized her book, *Rival Prima Donnas*, and prevailed upon a theatrical manager to produce it. The man who had her play in charge, however, neglected to fulfil his part of the bargain, and meanwhile, Louisa's ardor for the theatre cooled off.

By the time she was twenty-one, Miss Alcott was fairly launched as an author. Two years later she published a book, entitled *Flower Fables*, receiving from its sale the astonishing sum of thirty-two dollars. Then her work began to be accepted by the *Atlantic Monthly* and by other magazines of good standing.

It was very difficult for her to write in Concord, where she continually saw so much to be done at home. When a book was in process of writing she would go to Boston, hire a quiet room, and shut herself in until the work was completed. Then she would return to Concord to rest, "tired, hungry and cross," as she expressed it. While in Boston she worked cruelly hard, often writing fourteen hours out of the twenty-four. Worn out in body, she would grow discouraged and lose hope, wondering if she would ever be able to earn enough money to support her parents.

A dear and good friend of hers was the Reverend Theodore Parker. At his home the tired, anxious girl was certain to receive encouragement and cheer. There she met Emerson, Sumner, Garrison, Julia Ward Howe, and other eminent men and women of the time. A few years before her death she wrote to a friend:

> Theodore Parker and Ralph Emerson have done much to help me see that one can shape life best by trying to build up a strong and noble character through good books, wise people's society, and by taking an interest in all the reforms that help the world.

While in Boston Miss Alcott found time to go to teach in an evening Charity School. In her diary we find these jottings:

> I'll help, as I am helped, if I can.
> Mother says no one is so poor that he can't do a little for some one poorer yet.

At twenty-five years of age, Louisa Alcott was receiving not over five, six, or ten dollars for her stories. This would hardly support herself, to say nothing of the family.   Writing might be continued, but sewing and teaching could not be dropped.

In 1861, when the Civil War broke out, her natural love of action as well as her patriotism caused her to offer her services as nurse.   In December, 1862, she went to Washington where she was given a post in the Union Hospital at Georgetown.   The Alcott family had been full of courage until it was time for her to depart.   Then all broke down.   Louisa herself felt she was taking her life in her hands and that she might never come back.

She said, "Shall I stay, Mother?"

"No, no, go! and the Lord be with you," replied her mother, bravely smiling, and waving good-bye with a wet handkerchief.   So Louisa departed, depressed in spirits and with forebodings of trouble.

She found the hospital small, poorly ventilated, and crowded with patients.   Her heart was equal to the task, but her strength was not.

In her diary, she tells us the events of a day:

Up at six, dress by gas light, run through my ward and throw up the windows, though the men grumble and shiver; but the air is bad enough to breed a pestilence. Poke up the fire, add blankets, joke, coax, command; but I continue to open doors and windows as if life depended upon it.

Till noon I trot, trot, giving out rations, cutting up food for helpless boys, washing faces, teaching my attendants how beds are made, or floors are swept, dressing wounds, dusting tables, sewing bandages, keeping my tray tidy, rushing up and down after pillows, bed-linen, sponges, books, and directions till it seems I would joyfully pay all I possess for fifteen minutes' rest.

When dinner is over, some sleep, many read, and others want letters written. This I like to do, for they put in such odd things. The answering of letters from friends after some one has died is the saddest and hardest duty a nurse has to do.

After six weeks of nursing Miss Alcott fell seriously ill with typhoid-pneumonia.

As she refused to leave her duties, a friend sent word of her condition to her father, who came to the hospital and took her back with him to Concord. It was months before she recovered sufficiently even to continue her literary work, and never again was she robust in health. She writes: "I was never ill before I went to the hospital, and I have never been well since."

Her letters written home while she was nursing in Georgetown contained very graphic and accurate descriptions of hospital life. At the suggestion of her mother and sisters, Miss Alcott revised and added to these letters, making a book which she called

Hospital Sketches. This book met with instant success, and a part of the success was money.

After that, all was easy. There came requests from magazine editors offering from two to three hundred dollars for serials. Her place in the literary field being now an assured thing, her natural fondness for children led her to writing for them.

The series comprising *Little Women, Jo's Boys,* and *Little Men;* together with *An Old Fashioned Girl, Eight Cousins, Rose in Bloom, Under the Lilacs, Jack and Jill,* and many others, are books dear to the hearts of all children. Editions of all these books were published in England, and in several other European countries where translations had been made of them, — all of which brought in large royalties for the author.

What happiness it must have given her to make her family independent, and to be able to travel! Twice she visited Europe, the first time as companion to an invalid woman, and a second time, after she had earned enough to pay her own expenses.

Miss Alcott never married. When about twenty-five years of age, an offer of marriage came to her which most young women would have considered very flattering. But she did not love her suitor, and on her mother's advice, refused him, thus being saved from that worst of conditions — a loveless union.

This first offer was not the last Miss Alcott received and declined. Matrimony, she said, had no charms for her! She loved her family, and her literary work. Above all, she loved her freedom. Her health was not benefited by her second trip to Europe; excessive work had been too great a strain upon her, and her father's failing health demanded her constant care.

In 1877 Mrs. Alcott died, and in the autumn of 1882 Mr. Alcott had a stroke of paralysis. From this he never fully recovered. Louisa was his constant nurse, and it gave her great happiness to be able to gratify his every wish. About this time Orchard House, which had been the family home for twenty-five years, was sold, and the family went to live with Mrs. Pratt, the eldest daughter.

Hoping that an entire change of air and scene might help her father, Miss Alcott rented a fine house in Louisburg Square, Boston, to which she had him removed. Here she showed him every attention, until her own health became so impaired that she was obliged to go to the home of Dr. Lawrence, at Roxbury, for medical care.

A few days before her death, she was taken to see her dying father. Shortly after her visit he passed away, and three days later she followed him. Born on her father's birthday, she died on the day he was buried, March 6, 1888.

All her life Louisa Alcott labored to make others happy, and she is still reaping her harvest of love the world over.

FRANCES WILLARD

FRANCES E. WILLARD

(1839 – 1898)

"There is a woman at the beginning of all great things."
— *Alphonse de Lamartine*

It was not until 1873 that the vast amount of drunkenness in our country attracted the attention of the women of America.

A crusade was formed against it in the West, and this led in 1874 to the foundation of the Women's Christian Temperance Union. Frances Elizabeth Willard was offered the position of president, an honor she then declined, preferring to work in the ranks; but four years later she yielded to the universal demand, and accepted the chairmanship of this great movement.

This able woman was born at Churchville, very near Rochester, N. Y., on September 28, 1839. Her father, of English descent, was a man of intellectual force, brave, God-fearing; her mother, a woman of strong religious feeling, great courage, and of fine mental equipment. Frances inherited the best quali-

199

ties of both parents.   When she was two years of age, the family removed to Oberlin, Ohio, and about five years later to Janesville, Wisconsin, then almost a wilderness.   Here they lived the simple, hard life of pioneers.   Frances was at first taught by her mother and a governess; afterward, she and her younger sister entered the Northwestern College at Evanston, from which Frances was graduated.

Mr. Willard removed to Evanston in order to be near his daughters while they were in college, and in 1858 built a house there.   Here the younger daughter died, and later Mr. Willard, but Frances and her mother continued to make it their home, even after the death of the only son.   Frances named it Rest Cottage, and here she returned each year of her busy life to spend two months with the mother whom she had christened St. Courageous.

Idleness was an impossibility for Frances Willard. After her graduation she taught in a little district school, and from 1858 until 1868 continued the work of teaching in various schools and colleges.   In 1868 she went to Europe and spent two years in travel and study.   Upon her return she was elected President of the Evanston College for Women, being the first woman in the world to hold such a position.

Two years later, when the college became a part of the Northwestern University, Miss Willard became Dean of the Women's College, but as some of her views conflicted with those of the President, she soon resigned the position.

It was about this time that the women of Ohio began fighting the liquor traffic. To use Mrs. Livermore's words, "Frances Willard caught the spirit of the Woman's Crusade and believed herself called of God to take up the temperance cause as her life work."

Every one, even her mother, opposed her, but feeling herself called to the work she gave to it all her energies of heart and soul.

When Miss Willard became President of the Women's Christian Temperance Union in 1879, the yearly income of the Union was only twelve hundred dollars. The movement was too new and too strange to command much understanding or sympathy from the public; the work, so far, had been done without system. Frances Willard at once began to put the machinery in order: she organized bodies of workers and lecturers; she instituted relief work and educative centers; and the numbers of these she constantly increased.

Perhaps Miss Willard's greatest moral asset was

the power of winning followers. Many, many women rallied enthusiastically to her support and helped her to carry out her plans. To zeal and intelligence she added charming manners and eloquence. As a leader her ability was marvelous. Love came to her from all sides because love went out from her to everybody.

Her own love of the work was so great that for years she labored without a salary, for the Union had hard struggles to live even after Miss Willard undertook the leadership of it. But with or without salary, never did she spare herself.

It is said that during the first two years of her work she delivered on an average one speech a day on temperance and other reforms. She visited every town in the United States of over ten thousand inhabitants and most of those above five thousand.

The next step in Miss Willard's progress was a very great one; no less a thing than the organization of a World's Women's Christian Temperance Union! Yes, this courageous and enterprising woman actually planned to carry her crusade against strong drink into every corner of the globe. At the Columbian Exposition in Chicago in 1893 she was chosen Chairman of the World's Temperance Convention.

Meanwhile, Lady Henry Somerset, a charming
and brilliant Englishwoman who had been working
in her own country to secure the same reforms Miss
Willard was pushing forward in America, came to
this country. It was her first visit — made, she
said, less to see America than to see Miss. Willard,
and learn from her the principle upon which she had
founded the marvelous organization.

These two noble women became devoted friends,
and when, in the autumn of 1892, Lady Henry again
came to America to attend a National Convention
at Denver, she persuaded Miss Willard to return with
her to England. Our great temperance leader had a
fine reception from the English people, and won all
hearts by her gentleness and earnestness, as well as
by her remarkable gift of oratory.

Four years after this, the World's Women's Christian Temperance Union held a Convention in London.
Every country in the civilized world sent delegates
to this meeting, over which Miss Willard and
Lady Somerset presided. These indefatigable world-
workers had secured a petition of seven million
names. It encircled the entire hall of the Convention, and besides lay in large rolls on the platform.
This petition asked of all governments to have the

sale of intoxicating liquors and of opium restricted. But, in spite of the seven million signatures and an enormous enthusiasm, the sale of liquors and drugs went on as before. Yet something was accomplished: a great increase of sympathy in public opinion.

In addition to all these activities Miss Willard was much engaged in literary work. She acted as editor on various papers and magazines; also she wrote several books, *Nineteen Beautiful Years*, *Glimpses of Fifty Years*, *Woman and Temperance*, being the best known.

When the White Cross and White Shield movements for the promotion of social purity were formed, Miss Willard, as leader, did a glorious work. Under the white flag of the Women's Christian Temperance Union with its famous motto, *For God, for Home and Native Land*, she brought together, to work as sisters, the women of the South and the North.

Miss Willard was always dignified, earnest, and inspiring, but when talking on the subject so dear to her heart she grew eloquent. As a presiding officer, justice, tact, grace, and quick repartee made her the ideal platform speaker, though, perhaps, courage may be called her chief characteristic.

In later years, although suffering from ill health,

she yet kept cheerfully at work and actually presided over the Convention of 1897.   This, however, proved too great a strain, and on February 18, 1898, at the Empire Hotel, New York City, she died.   Her body died, but her soul "goes marching on."

MARTHA WASHINGTON

WOMEN IN PIONEER LIFE AND ON THE BATTLE-FIELD

"If we wish to know the political and moral condition of a State, we must ask what rank women hold in it. Their influence embraces the whole of life."

— *Aimé Martin*

The first foot that pressed Plymouth Rock was that of Mary Chilton, a fair and delicate maiden, and there followed her eighteen women who had accompanied their husbands on the Mayflower to the bleak, unknown shore of Massachusetts. Truly the "spindle side" of the Puritan stock deserves great admiration and respect.

These women came from a civilized land to a savage one; from homes of plenty, where they had been carefully guarded and tended, to a place where their lives could be only danger, toil and privation. Often they were obliged to pound corn for their bread, and many were the times, their husbands being away fighting the Indians, when they gathered their children together, panic-stricken by the war whoops that rang out from the wilderness near by. Little wonder that four of these eighteen women died during the first winter, killed by cold, hunger, and mental anguish!

The early European settlers of America, both men and women, were of a truly heroic breed. It' was spiritual as well as bodily courage they displayed — suffering as they did for a religious principle. The women often performed the duties of men, even planting the crops in their husbands' absence, and frequently using firearms to guard their children and their homes. Shoulder to shoulder with the men these women worked, and from the struggle was evolved a new type — the woman of 1776, without whose assistance the Revolutionary War could scarcely have succeeded.

One of these women, who might have lived in luxury, aloof from scenes of suffering, had she so wished, stands out prominently. This was Martha Washington, the wife of the Commander-in-Chief of the Continental Army, who gathered the wives of the officers around her at Valley Forge, during the severe winter of 1777–78, and with them undertook the work of relieving the needs of the soldiers. Under her leadership the women gave up their embroidery, spinnet playing, and other light accomplishments, and knitted stockings and mittens, of which hundreds of pairs were distributed.   We may regard her as the pioneer in a form of work which later developed into Sanitary Commissions and the great organization of the Red Cross.

A different type of woman was Moll Pitcher.   She showed her courage in quite another way.   She was the wife of John Hayes, a gunner.   At that time, a few married women, who found it easier to stand the fearful strain of battle than to remain at home in suspense, waiting for news of it, were allowed to accompany their husbands to the battle-field, — not to fight — oh, no, but to wash, and mend, and cook for the men.   Moll was one of these.

During the Battle of Monmouth, *Moll o' the Pitcher*, as she was called, because of the stone pitcher she used in carrying water to the soldiers, was engaged in her usual work when she saw her husband fall by the side of his gun.   Running to him, she helped him to a place of safety; then, at his request, she returned to his gun.   The commander was just about to have it taken from the field, but as Moll offered her services, he allowed it to remain.   She managed it so well that the report of her prowess spread, even to the ears of General Washington. The General called upon her to thank her, and the Continental Congress gave her a sergeant's commis-

MOLLY PITCHER

sion and half-pay for life. "Captain Mollie," done with military service, took her wounded husband home and nursed him, but he died of his wounds before the war closed.

Lydia Darrah, a Quakeress of Philadelphia, by her quick wit and courage saved General Washington's army from capture at Whitemarsh after the defeat at Germantown. During the winter of 1777 the British commander, General Howe, had his head-quarters in Second Street. Directly opposite dwelt William and Lydia Darrah, strict Quakers whose religion debarred them from taking sides in the war. Because of this, perhaps, the British officers considered their home a safe place for private meetings, a large, rear room in the house being frequently used for conferences with the staff-officers.

One evening, the Adjutant General told Lydia that they would be there until late, but that he wished the family to retire early, adding that, when the conference was over he would call her to let them out and put out the lights. Lydia obeyed, but could not sleep. Her intuition told her that something of importance to Washington was being discussed. Try as she might to be neutral, as a Quaker should, her sympathies were with the great General.

At last she slipped from her bed, crept to the door of the meeting-room, and listened at the keyhole. She heard an order read for all British troops to march out on the evening of December fourth to capture Washington's army, which was then encamped at Whitemarsh. Frightened and excited, she returned to her room.

Not long after, the officer knocked at her door, but she pretended to be asleep and did not answer. As the knocking continued, she finally opened the door and sleepily returned the officer's good night. Then she locked up the house and put out the lights, but spent the remainder of the night in thinking over what she should do. Early next morning she told her husband that their flour was all gone and she would have to go to the mill at Franklin, five miles away, to get more.

She presented herself at the British headquarters bright and early, asking permission to pass through the lines on a domestic errand. Permission was granted, and she started for Franklin. She did not stop there, however, but leaving her bag to be filled ready for her upon her return, she continued walking until she reached the American outposts. Asking that she might speak to an officer, she told what she had heard, begging that she might not be betrayed. Then she hastened back to the mill, secured her bag of flour and returned home as if nothing had happened.

And so it came about that, when the British reached Whitemarsh, they found the American Army, which they had planned to surprise, drawn up in line awaiting battle. No battle took place; but the British returned to Philadelphia, and there tried to find out who had betrayed their plans. Lydia Darrah was called up and questioned. She said that the members of her family were all in bed at eight o'clock on the night of the conference.

"It is strange," said the officer; "I know that you were sound asleep, for I had to knock several times to awaken you."

So the matter was dropped, and nobody knows to this day whether the British ever learned the truth or not.

The story of Emily Geiger's bravery has been told in prose and poetry many times. It became necessary for General Green to get reinforcements from General Sumter. The latter was about fifty miles away, and the country between them was overrun with British soldiers. When Emily heard that General Green needed a messenger for the dangerous journey, she immediately offered her services. Well she knew that discovery would mean being hanged for a spy, but the risk did not appal her. Rather unwillingly the General consented to her entreaties, and entrusted the letter to her, telling her its contents in case it should by any chance get lost. A woman, he said, *might* run a chance of getting past the British soldiers when a man would surely fail.

"I have a fleet horse," said Emily, "which I broke and trained myself; I know the country and I am sure I can get through." She dashed away, but was captured on the second day and imprisoned in a room of an old farm-house.

As soon as she was alone, she tore the letter up, and chewed and swallowed the pieces. This was done none too soon, for immediately afterward, a woman entered and Emily had to submit to being searched. Nothing of a suspicious nature being found upon her, the British allowed her to go on. Before sundown Emily reached General Sumter's camp and delivered the message. As a result, after a hard fought battle at Eutaw Springs, the British were defeated by General Green. Emily Geiger married happily and lived to a good old age. Long should she be remembered for her courage and patriotism.

It is certain that at least one woman enlisted in the Continental Army and fought as a soldier in the Revolutionary War. This woman was Deborah Samson, the daughter of poor parents of Plymouth County, Massachusetts. She was but twenty-two years of age when she left home, adopted male attire, and enlisted under the name of Robert Shirtliffe.

A flaxen-haired girl was Deborah, with blue eyes and rosy cheeks; she was not pretty, although as a man she might have passed for handsome. Accustomed from childhood to do farm work, she had acquired the vigor and strength that enabled her to perform the trying duties of military life. Deborah saw something of real war. At White Plains she received two bullet holes in her coat and one in her cap; at Yorktown she went through a severe fight but came out unhurt. Once she was shot in the thigh, but fear of discovery exceeded the pain of the wound, and she refused to go to the hospital. Later she fell ill of brain fever, and in the hospital her sex was discovered by the doctor. He did not betray her, but as soon as her health permitted he had her removed to his own house, where he gave her every care.

When her health was restored, the physician had a conference with the Commander of the Regiment to which "Robert" belonged. Soon there followed an order to the young man to carry a letter to Washington. Our young soldier felt very uneasy, but a soldier must obey. In due time, she appeared before General Washington. With great delicacy the General said not a word to her regarding the letter she had brought, but handed one, Robert Shirtliffe, a discharge from the army, and a note containing a few words of advice, with sufficient money to pay her expenses until she could find a home.

Deborah then resumed woman's attire and returned to her family. At the close of the war she married Benjamin Gannet of Sharon. While Washington was President, he invited Deborah to visit the capital. She accepted, and during her stay there Congress passed a bill granting her a pension for the services she had rendered the country.

It has been stated, and is doubtless true, that many women, disguised as men, enlisted during the Civil War and served as soldiers. Others followed the army as nurses, fighting when it became necessary. Many of these women went because they could not bear the separation from their husbands. A notable example of this class was Madame Turchin, wife of the Colonel of the Nineteenth Illinois. She was the daughter of a Russian officer and had always lived in foreign camps with her father. During the War of the Rebellion, she accompanied her husband to the battle-field and became a great favorite with the soldiers under his command. To her the men went when they were ill or in any trouble, knowing they would always meet with sympathy, and when necessary would be given careful nursing.

Upon one occasion, when the regiment was actively engaged in Tennessee, Col. Turchin fell ill, having to be carried for several days in an ambulance. His wife took the most tender care of him, and also assumed his place at the head of the regiment, even leading the troops into action. Officers and men in the ranks alike obeyed her, for her courage and skill equaled those of her husband. Without faltering she faced the hottest fire. When her husband recovered and again took command, she retired to the rear and resumed the work of nursing the sick and wounded.

Like Madame Turchin, Mrs. Kady Brownell had been accustomed to camp life, her father having been a soldier in the British Army. She married an officer of the Fifth Rhode Island Infantry and accompanied him to the front. She bore the regimental colors and marched with the men, asking no favors and standing the brunt of battle fearlessly. A fine shot was Mrs. Kady Brownell, also an expert in the use of the sword. She was in General Burnside's expedition to Roanoke Island and Newburn. There her husband was so seriously wounded that he was judged unfit for further service and given his discharge. Mrs. Brownell asked for a discharge likewise, and together they retired to private life.

Annie Etheridge of Michigan is said to have been with the Third Michigan in every battle in which it was engaged. When the three years of its service was over, she followed the re-enlisted veterans to the Fifth Michigan. Through the entire four years of war, this fearless woman never left the field, though often under the hottest fire. She made herself beloved and respected by both officers and men.

Bridget Devins, known as "Michigan Bridget," because she went to the front with the First Michigan Cavalry, in which her husband served as private, was noted for her daring deeds and her good service. When the troops were about to retreat, it was Michigan Bridget who rallied them. When a soldier fell, she took his place, fighting bravely in his stead. Often she carried the wounded from the field, risking her own life in the performance of her duty.   Michigan Bridget liked military life so well that at the close of the war she and her husband joined the regular army and were sent to a station on the western plains.

These women soldiers who served so bravely on the field of battle, we must honor, yet we cannot regret that their numbers were small.   The nobler service of those countless women, who, with white faces and breaking hearts, sent to the front their husbands, fathers and sons, can never be properly estimated nor sufficiently honored.

These women toiled day and night, determined that the soldiers should be well cared for and well fed; they organized relief work so that the fighters might have comforts and good hospitals.   These women as truly enlisted for battle as did the others who went to the front.

WS - #0210 - 111124 - C0 - 229/152/13 - PB - 9781330328804 - Gloss Lamination